2012
DOOMSDAY PLANNER

THE
OFFICIAL UNAUTHORIZED MAKEOVER
OF THE MAYAN CALENDAR

by L.K. Peterson and Martin Kozlowski
Illustrated by Martin Kozlowski

Special thanks to Paul Kozlowski for his guidance and encouragement, Jana Kozlowski for her
Mother's Day artwork, and Deborah & Barbara for their patience and support.

For updates on the approaching doom visit 2012doomsdayplanner.com.

2012

DOOMSDAY PLANNER

THE LONG COUNT GOODBYE

The Mayans don't say what happens on December 21, 2012, the date their 5,126-year-long calendar abruptly ends, and this puzzling omission has kept scholars, prophets and doomsday book publishers in business for decades.

The Mayan Long Count calendar measures time using interconnected and overlapping systems of solar and lunar cycles, numerically defined periods of days, months and millennia, then synchronizes them with the alignment of the stars and the harmonizing of spiritual, mythological, zodiacal forces along with the occasional three-day weekend.

Got it? Neither do we. That's why we went back through the Mayan's calendar and reinterpreted and revised it glyph by glyph, from beginning to end.

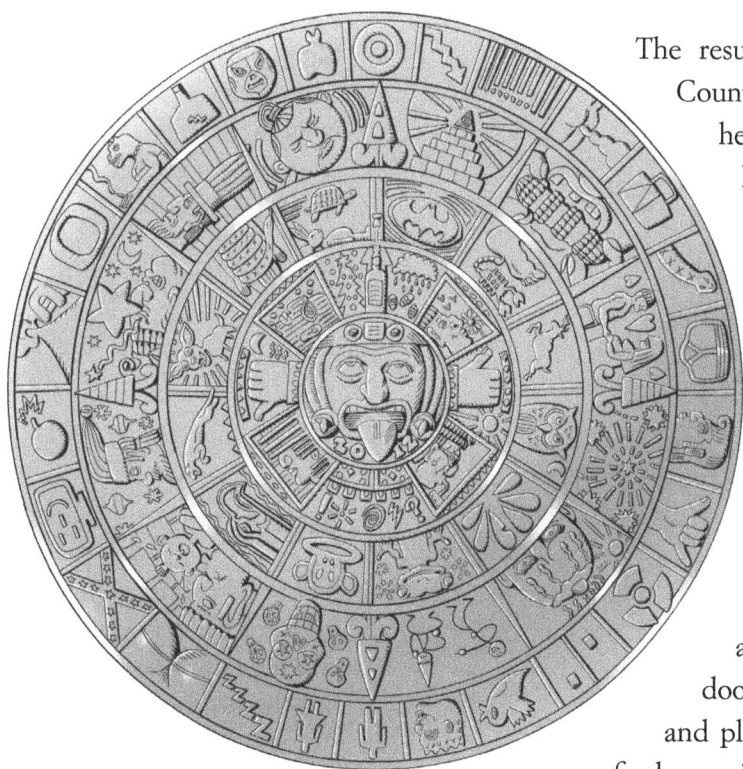

The result is the Mayan "Dozen Count" calendar, presented here as the 2012 Doomsday Planner. Compressed into a user-friendly 12-month format, it offers several improvements on the original, not the least of which is that it's no longer a 12-foot tall chunk of stone weighing 25 tons. It also offers a glimpse into Mayan customs and culture, a survey of doomsday predictions past, and plenty of room to pencil in final appointments, farewell parties and serve your every countdown scheduling need right up to December 21.

After that? You didn't really think we'd give away the ending, did you?

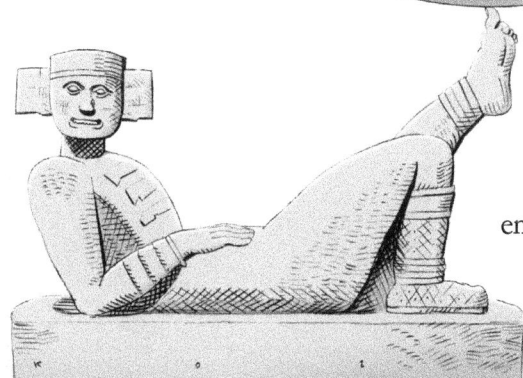

THE FOUR SEASONS

The Mayans divided their year into four distinct seasons and used their prognosticating calendar as an almanac by which to schedule the planting of crops, coordinate their hectic lineup of festivals and place bets on sporting events. Many Mayans loved the Four Seasons, although some preferred the Four Tops.

WINTER

There's no Mayan word for snow and they didn't need one. Yucatan winters are like Florida in February, but with wa-a-a-y fewer old people. The Mayans might have heard about cold weather from Incas who'd wandered up from the Andes, but they probably didn't believe them.

SPRING

Most of this brief shoulder season between the dry period just ended and the rainy season about to begin was devoted to patching roofs and making sacrifices to the trickster water sprite **Le'ek**, god of waterproofing.

Glyph Notes

The godhead in the calendar's center is surrounded by four avatars of the seasons. These are ringed by twelve zodiacal animals, a dozen monthly glyphs and, finally, twenty-six fortnightly glyphs. Explanations of the glyphs' iconography are provided throughout the dayplanner. A quiz on the nature of the totem animals follows on the next page.

Summer

Daily weather forecasts for the Yucatan May through mid-September are predictable and consistent: Rain, followed by sweltering humidity, then by more rain. This pattern repeated itself hourly until the hurricane season started.

Autumn

Once hurricane season ended, Mayans who hadn't been hurled to Oaxaca harvested crops and prepared offerings to **D'lan**, spirit god of the blowing wind. They hoped to appease the enigmatic deity into mumbling an answer to the age-old question, "What's with the hurricanes, already?"

WHAT'S YOUR MAYAN TOTEM ANIMAL?

1. Someone is between you and your goal; do you...
   a) Pounce on them, rip their throat out and proceed.
   b) Hump their leg until you get what you want.
   c) Stare at them blankly while they run you over with their car.

2. In your spare time you like to...
   a) Conquer neighboring tribes.
   b) Scamper up and down ancient ruins.
   c) Make feathered headdresses.

3. You enter a room where you don't know anyone; what do you do first?
   a) Find the weakest in the crowd and eat them.
   b) Establish your dominance through a series of flailing motions and shrieking cries.
   c) Strut your plumage until someone notices, then, if nobody does, leave in a huff.

4. If you could choose where to live, where would it be?
   a) On high ground, with good sight lines.
   b) Somewhere with lots of cover; tall grass, say.
   c) Anyplace cozy, preferably pink.

5. Which description fits you best?
   a) Cold-blooded.
   b) Easygoing.
   c) Warm 'n' fuzzy.

6. If this quiz shows you're not the Mayan totem animal you wanted to be, you will:
   a) Eat something huge, then spend the next week digesting it.
   b) Sting somebody. *Anybody.*
   c) Hug everyone and make new friends.

Scoring: Each "a" answer is worth 3 points; each "b" is worth 2 points; each "c" is 1 point. If you answered "yes" or "no" to any of the questions, you're:
a) Taking the wrong quiz; b) Not paying attention; c) Really need new glasses.

Your Score: 18 Jaguar; 17 Scorpion; 16 Hawk; 15 Snake;
14 Monkey; 13 Bat; 12 Owl; 11 Dog; 10 Turtle;
9 Lizard; 8 Rabbit; 7 Deer; 6 Peacock; 0-5 Hello Kitty

AND YOUR MAYAN TOTEM ANIMAL IS

18 The Jaguar — You are quick, sleek and deadly, but also ridiculously overpriced and expensive to repair.

17 The Scorpion — The threat of your deadly sting keeps your enemies away. And everyone else. You don't get invited out much.

16 The Hawk — You are a soaring hunter with sharp eyesight, then again, you hunt small rodents.

15 The Snake — You are graceful in a slithery sort of way; you'd make a great matching belt, shoes and handbag.

14 The Monkey — You are curious, energetic and clever. You also throw your own feces when provoked and sometimes for no reason at all.

13 The Bat — Your radar is truly amazing, but it doesn't begin to make up for the overall creepiness.

12 The Owl — You are wise enough to come out only at night; the right choice, given your looks.

11 The Dog — *Who's* a good totem animal? *Who's* a good totem animal? *You* are! *Yes*, you are!

10 The Turtle — When you do come out of your shell, it's rarely worth the wait. What, do you have premium cable in there?

9 The Lizard — Miraculous as it may be that it always grows back, your party trick, "Pull my tail off!" is getting a little tiresome.

8 The Rabbit — You handily evade stuttering hunters with your hilarious wisecracks, but the cross-dressing is beginning to raise eyebrows.

7 The Deer — While you look majestic and noble, your repeated attempts to stare down approaching car headlights indicates that you're a bit of a slow learner.

6 The Peacock — Beautiful, yes, but nobody likes a showoff.

0-5 Hello Kitty — You don't have a Mayan totem animal. Check with the Aztecs, maybe they've got something for you.

JAGUAR

SCORPION

HAWK

SNAKE

MONKEY

BAT

OWL

DOG

LIZARD

RABBIT & TURTLE

DEER

PEACOCK

2012: The Last Year

January

S	M	T	W	T	F	S
1	2	3	4	5	6	7
8	9	10	11	12	13	14
15	16	17	18	19	20	21
22	23	24	25	26	27	28
29	30	31				

February

S	M	T	W	T	F	S
			1	2	3	4
5	6	7	8	9	10	11
12	13	14	15	16	17	18
19	20	21	22	23	24	25
26	27	28	29			

March

S	M	T	W	T	F	S
				1	2	3
4	5	6	7	8	9	10
11	12	13	14	15	16	17
18	19	20	21	22	23	24
25	26	27	28	29	30	31

April

S	M	T	W	T	F	S
1	2	3	4	5	6	7
8	9	10	11	12	13	14
15	16	17	18	19	20	21
22	23	24	25	26	27	28
29	30					

May

S	M	T	W	T	F	S
		1	2	4	4	5
6	7	8	9	10	11	12
13	14	15	16	17	18	19
20	21	22	23	24	25	26
27	28	29	30	31		

June

S	M	T	W	T	F	S
					1	2
3	4	5	6	7	8	9
10	11	12	13	14	15	16
17	18	19	20	21	22	23
24	25	26	27	28	29	30

July

S	M	T	W	T	F	S
1	2	3	4	5	6	7
8	9	10	11	12	13	14
15	16	17	18	19	20	21
22	23	24	25	26	27	28
29	30	31				

August

S	M	T	W	T	F	S
			1	2	3	4
5	6	7	8	9	10	11
12	13	14	15	16	17	18
19	20	21	22	23	24	25
26	27	28	29	30	31	

September

S	M	T	W	T	F	S
						1
2	3	4	5	6	7	8
9	10	11	12	13	14	15
16	17	18	19	20	21	22
23	24	25	26	27	28	29
30						

October

S	M	T	W	T	F	S
	1	2	3	4	5	6
7	8	9	10	11	12	13
14	15	16	17	18	19	20
21	22	23	24	25	26	27
28	29	30	31			

November

S	M	T	W	T	F	S
				1	2	3
4	5	6	7	8	9	10
11	12	13	14	15	16	17
18	19	20	21	22	23	24
25	26	27	28	29	30	

December

S	M	T	W	T	F	S
						1
2	3	4	5	6	7	8
9	10	11	12	13	14	15
16	17	18	19	20	21	22
23	24	25	26	27	28	29
30	31					

2012
DOOMSDAY PLANNER

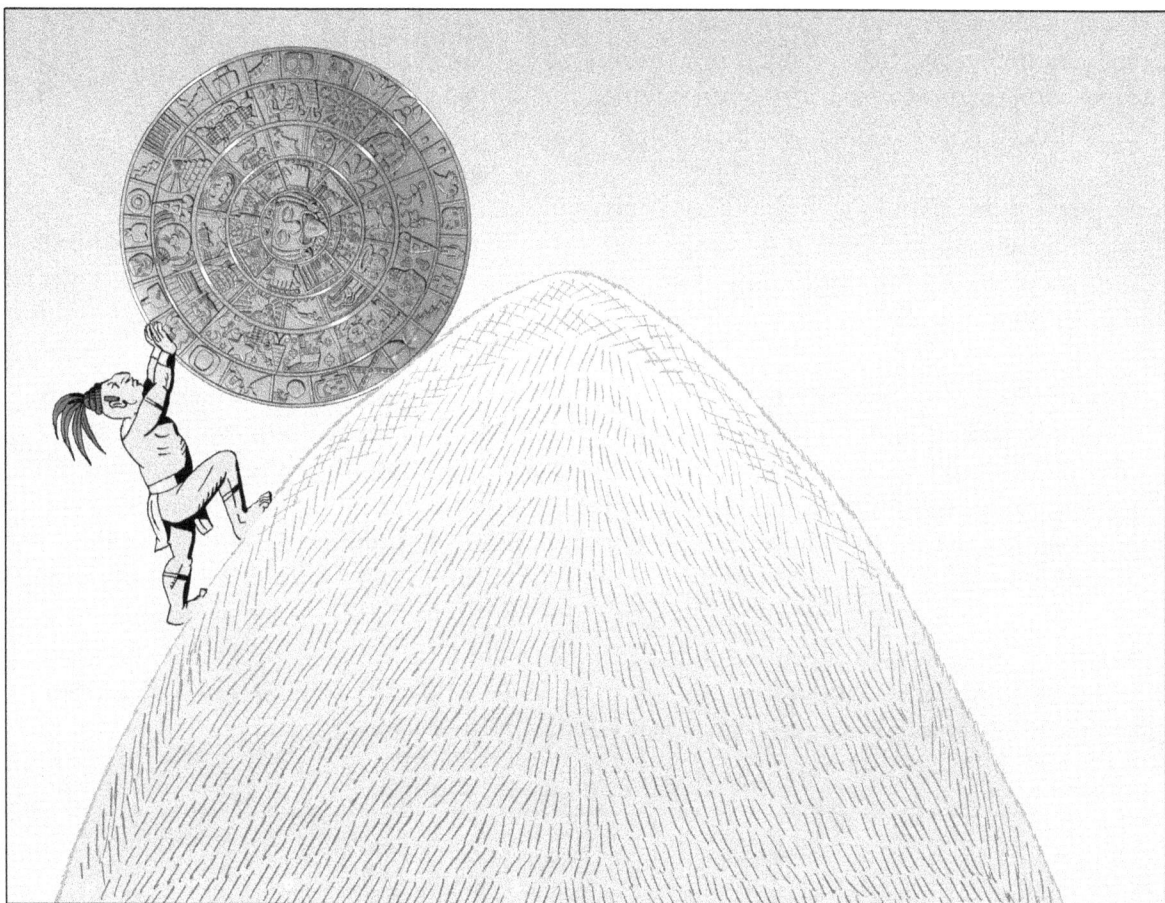

WEEK BY WEEK
DATEBOOK

SPACE CASES

The Mayan calendar's prophetic credibility comes largely from its uncannily precise astronomical forecasts. With pinpoint accuracy, the calendar has predicted — centuries in advance — every full moon, solar eclipse and the exact positions at any moment of Venus, Mars and Uranus.* It also foretold not only each and every reappearance of Halley's Comet, but the 1952 formation of Bill Haley and the Comets.

So how did the Maya — who had the wheel but didn't know what to do with it — come up with such advanced celestial insights? New evidence

P'PRAZI, THE ORIGINAL STAR-GAZER

suggests that they may have had some otherworldly help with their astronomy homework.

Satellite imagery of the Observatorio at Xochicalco reveals what looks like the diagram for an interstellar landing zone. Extraterrestrial visitation would go a long way in explaining the Mayans' detailed knowledge of outer space as well as why the observatory has arrival gates, baggage claim and a VIP lounge. This theory is further supported by adjacent archaeological digs that have unearthed a cluster of pre-Columbian conference centers, budget motels and duty-free shops.

Mayan historical records document periodic stopovers made by those referred to by a phrase that translates as either "sky visitors" or "those freeloading bastards who never pick up a check and there's always a lot less tequila after they leave … we're just saying."

*Scholars note that all Mayan references to the position of this last planet are invariably followed by the notation, "It's right behind you! HA HA! Gotcha again!"

J'X

G'GA

B'UUZI

PROOF OF ALIEN VISITATIONS?

JANUARY

S	M	T	W	T	F	S
1	2	3	4	5	6	7
8	9	10	11	12	13	14
15	16	17	18	19	20	21
22	23	24	25	26	27	28
29	30	31				

DOOMSDATES OF FUTURE PASSED

Y2K; in the year 2000, many people believed computers worldwide would stop functioning because they weren't programmed to deal with years that didn't start with "19". The fact that computers worldwide routinely stop functioning several times every day and can usually be coaxed back into usefulness by hitting "restart" did little to calm frayed Millennial nerves.

THE FORTNIGHTLY GLYPH

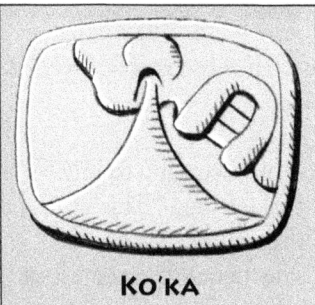

KO'KA

Symbol of the only demi-god more jittery than the caffeinated **Mo'ka.**

360

monday
26
Boxing Day Canada
Memo: Put away the Christmas lights, eh?
362

361

tuesday
27
361

362

wednesday
28
360

363

thursday
29
359

364

friday
30
358

365

saturday
31
357

1

sunday
1
Happy Last Year!
356

SORRY, SORRY NIGHT

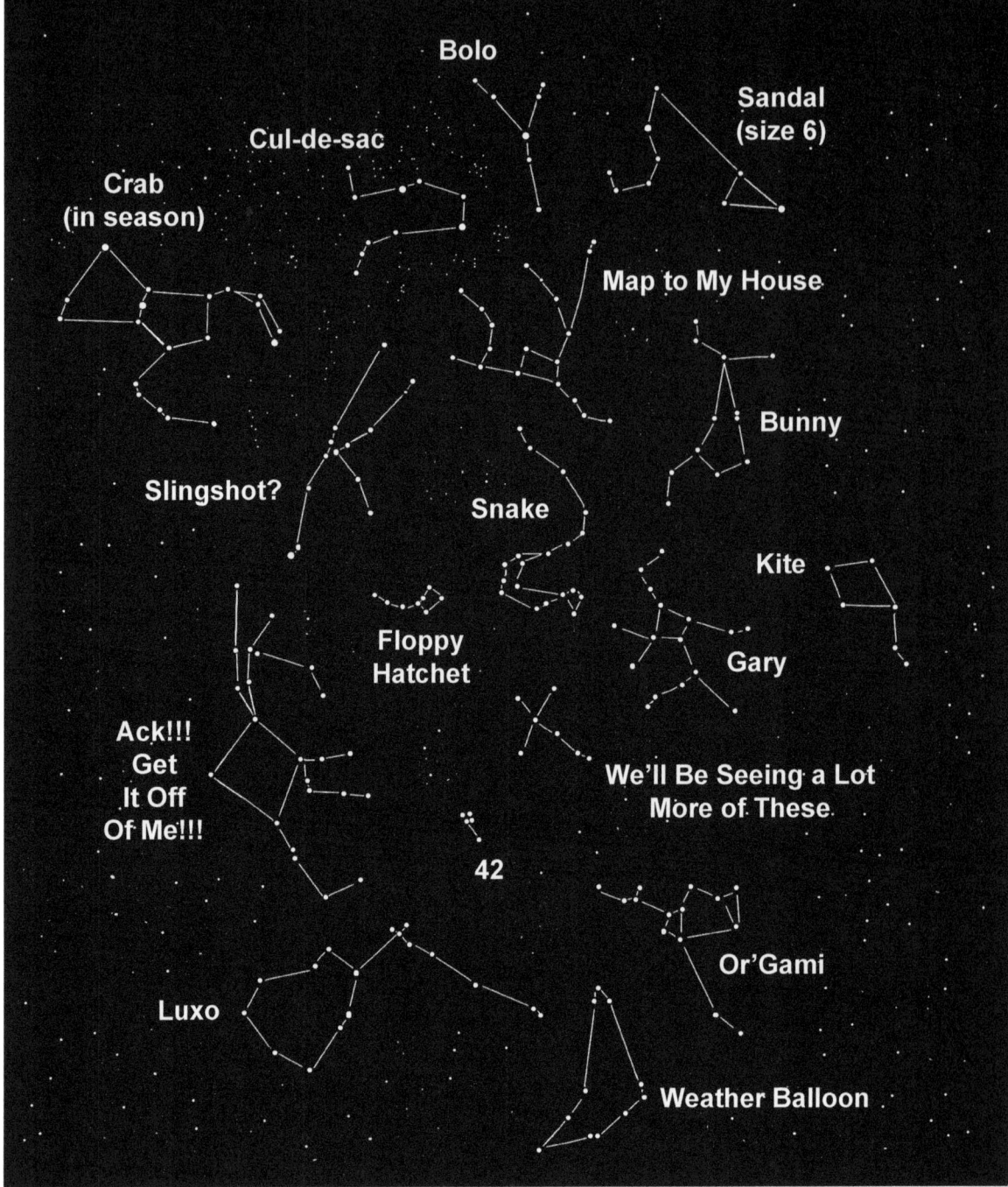

Bolo

Sandal
(size 6)

Cul-de-sac

Crab
(in season)

Map to My House

Bunny

Slingshot?

Snake

Kite

Floppy
Hatchet

Gary

Ack!!!
Get
It Off
Of Me!!!

We'll Be Seeing a Lot
More of These

42

Or'Gami

Luxo

Weather Balloon

Even though they'd shared a good laugh with visiting extraterrestrials over what those stupid Greeks called the constellations, the Mayans did their share of whimsical star naming.

In about 150 BCE, the renowned shaman/astronomer el Bondigas celebrated his ascension to high priest with a three day weekend-long, tequila and hallucinogen-fueled "spiritual journey." This event resulted in a wicked hangover, some awesome tattoos, at least two children and a "vision" of Quetzalcoatl, during which the Mayan god revealed the hidden shapes and true names of certain (but suspiciously not all) visible star systems. Despite some doubters, these designations were officially adopted and routinely used for the remainder of Mayan history.

JANUARY

DOOMSDATES OF FUTURE PASSED

There is some speculation that, because the Mayans appeared suddenly, from out of nowhere — a fully formed society — with extensive knowledge of time, space and advanced mathematics, then vanished just steps ahead of the conquistadors, they were themselves long-term extraterrestrial visitors. But that's just silly. Unless on their way out they crashed into the Bermuda Triangle...

2

monday

2

355

3

tuesday

3

354

Birthday of Mel Gibson

4

wednesday

4

353

5

thursday

5

352

Tweflth Night
Memo: Take down the dead tree already.

6

friday

6

351

Epiphany: This is the last year of the rest of my life!

7

saturday

7

350

8

sunday

8

349

JANURARY

HOW PEOPLE THINK WORLD WILL END

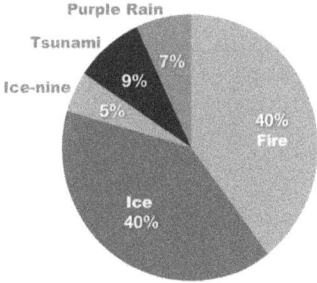

Purple Rain
Tsunami
Ice-nine

7%
9%
5%
40% Fire
Ice 40%

Marrieds 18-49

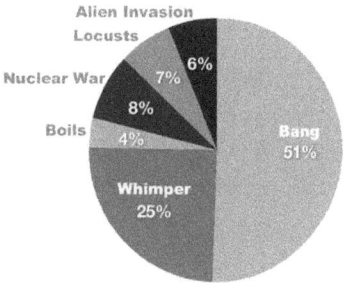

Alien Invasion
Locusts
Nuclear War
Boils

6%
7%
8%
4%
Bang 51%
Whimper 25%

Unmarrieds 18-49

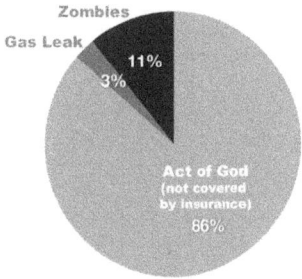

Zombies
Gas Leak

11%
3%
Act of God (not covered by insurance) 86%

Undecideds 18-49

9

monday

9

348

10

tuesday

10

347

Snow Day: Tell your teacher Nostradamus predicted it.

11

wednesday

11

346

12

thursday

12

345

13

friday

13

344

14

saturday

14

343

15

sunday

15

342

JANUARY

S	M	T	W	T	F	S
1	2	3	4	5	6	7
8	9	10	11	12	13	14
15	16	17	18	19	20	21
22	23	24	25	26	27	28
29	30	31				

Notes

THE FORTNIGHTLY GLYPH

O'PRA

All-seeing Goddess who showered her
worshippers with gifts and gab.

16

monday
16
341

Martin Luther King Jr. Day Observed

17

tuesday
17
340

18

wednesday
18
339

19

thursday
19
338

20

friday
20
337

21

saturday
21
336

22

sunday
22
335

January

S	M	T	W	T	F	S
1	2	3	4	5	6	7
8	9	10	11	12	13	14
15	16	17	18	19	20	21
22	23	24	25	26	27	28
29	30	31				

Notes

THIS WEEK IN MAYAN HISTORY

1113 A.D. The Mayans show off their latest innovations — pasta, gunpowder and supply-side economics — to visiting space aliens who tell them that the Chinese have already "been there, done that."

23

Chinese New Year: The Year of the Dragon
Memo: Sorry about the end of the world, what with this going to be your century and all.

monday
23
334

24

tuesday
24
333

25

wednesday
25
332

Halley's Comet appears, 66 A.D. — Mayans wave, Romans flip bird.

26

thursday
26
331

27

friday
27
330

28

saturday
28
329

29

sunday
29
328

ROYAL PAEANS

Every sizable Mayan city-state had its own king. These hereditary monarchs had reins that tended to be, like their lives and tempers, nasty, brutish and short.

Among the notable or notorious:

A'b: This early Mayan king was renowned for his honesty and was so beloved by his subjects that his image adorns the glyph symbolizing the winter month of his birth.

He was assassinated during the traditional *Our Mayan Cousin* pageant — which received decidedly mixed reviews — by a disgruntled actor jealous of his enormous headgear.

A'k'a: Ruled several city-states under different names.

A'dhoc: Known for his prioritizing and organizational skills and for focusing intently on one task at a time. He should have put "prevent overthrow" higher up on his to-do list.

K'chng: So openly corrupt he often bribed himself.

Sn'ak: "Old Avocado Breath"; is credited with the invention of the fish taco.

A'B

Sk'or: This charismatic ruler was quite the ladies' man; he "rescued" many a comely young maiden from virgin sacrifice by ensuring she no longer qualified.

E'go: Nearly bankrupted Chichen Itza building a pyramid to nowhere because he wanted to see the ocean from his tomb. Got his wish when he was whacked by unpaid contractors who dumped his corpse on a beach.

N'bred XVI: Last in a long line of increasingly ineffectual rulers, he was widely considered to be "a couple of feathers short of a headdress."

SN'AK

FEBRUARY

S	M	T	W	T	F	S
			1	2	3	4
5	6	7	8	9	10	11
12	13	14	15	16	17	18
19	20	21	22	23	24	25
26	27	28	29			

EROS IN JUDGMENT

On January 31, 433 Eros, the second largest Near Earth Object on record (size 8×8x20 miles), and the naughtiest, is expected to pass Earth at 0.1790 astronomical units (1 AU is roughly the distance from Earth to the sun). If it comes close enough to destroy us those Mayans will sure look silly, won't they?

DOOMSDATES OF FUTURE PASSED

On February 4, 1962, pop psychic/astrologer Jeanne Dixon said the Antichrist would be born the next day. It's probably a coincidence that February 5, 1962 is actress Jennifer Jason Leigh's birthday, but we should keep an eye on her.

30

monday
30
327

31

tuesday
31
326

32

wednesday
1
325

33

thursday
2
324

34

friday
3
323

35

saturday
4
322

36

sunday
5
321

Super Bowl XLVI
Memo: Consult entrails before placing bets.

DOOMSDAY FUNNIES

ZOMBIE

DOOMBERT

THE FAMINE CIRCUS

"No, we're out of Kitty Kat Bars —
this is Polly Onna Cracker."

THE FARCIDE

"Wow, it's so close even I could jump over it."

FEBRUARY

S	M	T	W	T	F	S
			1	2	3	4
5	6	7	8	9	10	11
12	13	14	15	16	17	18
19	20	21	22	23	24	25
26	27	28	29			

Notes

THE FORTNIGHTLY GLYPH

KOO'GA

Frisky feline demigoddess fond of
aged mezcal and young cats.

37

monday
6
320

Queen Elizabeth II's Diamond Jubilee commences —
promises to let Prince Charles wear crown for a day.

38

tuesday
7
319

Tu B'Shvat

39

wednesday
8
318

40

thursday
9
317

Halley's Comet, 1986 — Nancy Reagan's astrologer sees it as sign
that Just Say No policy will rid America of marijuana.

41

friday
10
316

Glenn Beck's Birthday

42

saturday
11
315

43

sunday
12
314

Abraham Lincoln's Birthday
And Ab's

FEBRUARY

S	M	T	W	T	F	S
			1	2	3	4
5	6	7	8	9	10	11
12	13	14	15	16	17	18
19	20	21	22	23	24	25
26	27	28	29			

Romantic Notions for your final V-Day

- Have your chakras aligned, your auras synchronized and your colons irrigated.

- Get intimate tattoos — Ixchel, the Goddess of Fertility for her, Ixnay, the God of ED for him.

- Play "alien abduction" with a pair of vibrating probes.

- Exchange gifts — a flame-retardant negligee for her, kevlar PJs for him.

- Stay up all night sipping pink champagne, and watch the sun rise languidly over your fallout shelter.

- Recite a romantic poem:
  Roses are red,
  Violets are blue,
  The end is near
  And so are you

- Promise to be true until the end of time (312 days and counting.)

44

monday
13
313

Presidents' Day

45

tuesday
14
312

Valentine's Day

46

wednesday
15
311

47

thursday
16
310

Halley's Comet, 374 — Oldest Mayan on record says, "not again."

48

friday
17
309

49

saturday
18
308

50

sunday
19
307

FEBRUARY

S	M	T	W	T	F	S
			1	2	3	4
5	6	7	8	9	10	11
12	13	14	15	16	17	18
19	20	21	22	23	24	25
26	27	28	29			

THIS WEEK IN MAYAN HISTORY

February 25, 2007
Although snubbed by Hollywood at the 2007 Academy Awards, Mel Gibson's *Apocalypto*, possibly the best Mayan-launguage film ever, receives "Best Cinematography" from the Central Ohio Film Critics Association, the Dallas-Fort Worth Film Critics Association and the Phoenix Film Critics Society as well as "Best Sound Editing" from the Motion Picture Sound Editors, USA and the Imagen Foundation Awards for "Best Supporting Actor" and "Best Supporting Actress". So, In Your Face, Oscar®!

51

monday
20
306

52

tuesday
21
305

Mardi Gras

53

wednesday
22
304

Ash Wednesday

54

thursday
23
303

55

friday
24
302

56

saturday
25
301

57

sunday
26
300

FEBRUARY

S	M	T	W	T	F	S
			1	2	3	4
5	6	7	8	9	10	11
12	13	14	15	16	17	18
19	20	21	22	23	24	25
26	27	28	29			

Notes

THE FORTNIGHTLY GLYPH

T'KILA

Spirit saluted on Fat Tuesday,
the day before "the worm turned."

58

monday

27
299

59

tuesday

28
298

Halley's Comet, 837 — Egbert of Wessex, first King of All England, swears off mead for a month.

60

wednesday

29
297

61

thursday

1
296

62

friday

2
295

63

saturday

3
294

64

sunday

4
293

MAYAN MARCH MADNESS

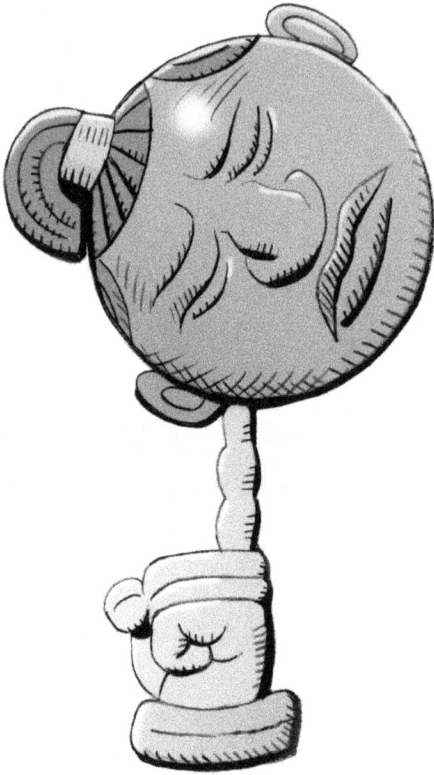

B'OL BOY

Mayans competed in a team sport called b'ol, about which little is known except that players could use only their hips and forearms to try putting a large rubber ball through a vertical loop set high on the courtside wall.

B'ol games were popular social events attended by anyone who could afford the season ticket prices. In the stands at any match were Mayans of every social rank, from chieftains, priests and dignitaries, right down to the players' wives.

Much like modern soccer, b'ol games could go on for several days before anything happened. When a team finally did manage to score, the crowds would erupt into a wild and thunderous frenzy, because it meant now they could all go home.

Winning teams received lavish victory celebrations and losing teams got executed, along with their mascot. Luckily, most teams had very effective farm systems; new recruits were simply grabbed off the nearest farm. Bidding wars over talented players were just that — wars.

Along with lives, fortunes could be lost at b'ol games as gambling on the outcome was not only allowed, but a huge part of the sport's appeal. Well-connected shamans were also bookies and often controlled arena concession stands as well. Ticket scalping, however, was illegal and the penalty for it severe; scalpers caught in the act were made the losing team's mascot.

Ruins of b'ol courts reveal an especially nasty centuries-long team rivalry between the powerhouse **Chichen Itza Chupacabras** and the perennial also-ran **Uxmal Monkeys**. In fact, the recent discovery of graffiti carved into the Chupacabras' home court by Uxmal fans opened up a whole new field of study in colloquial Mayan profanity.

BELOVED MASCOT C'HUPI

MARCH

7 HABITS OF HIGHLY SUCCESSFUL MAYANS

1: Set Realistic Goals

2: When Life Gives You Avocados, Make Guacamole

3: If you meet a stranger wearing a copper hat and looking for gold, tell him about that shiny fountain of youth over in Florida.

4: Keep Your Incas Close and Your Aztecs Closer

5: Remember, It's a Jungle Out There. No, Really, It's an Actual Jungle.

6: Happy Wife, Happy Life. Am I Right, Fellas?

7: Don't Be Around in the 16th Century.

65

monday

5

292

66

tuesday

6

291

67

wednesday

7

290

68

Purim

thursday

8

289

69

friday

9

288

70

saturday

10

287

71

Start of Daylight Savings Time — "Spring ahead" by advancing your watch by one hour or set it to midnight and remove the battery as a reminder of Doomsday's approach.

sunday

11

286

MARCH

S	M	T	W	T	F	S
				1	2	3
4	5	6	7	8	9	10
11	12	13	14	15	16	17
18	19	20	21	22	23	24
25	26	27	28	29	30	31

RAH RAH...

An archaeological dig near Chichen-Itza has unearthed what has been identified as the B'ol Hall of Fame Museum and Gift Shop.

Of the 50 ancient Maya cities currently mapped, about half of them are known to have had B'ol teams; more during the classical era. Sadly, however, only a handful of the original (and even fewer of the expansion) teams left any significant documentation.* This has fed speculation that, as Mayan civilization collapsed, many city states chose to take their dismal win/loss records with them.

Rumors that a B'ol team called the Tenochtitlan Lakers had been discovered at this site were recently proved to have been a hoax.

THE FORTNIGHTLY GLYPH

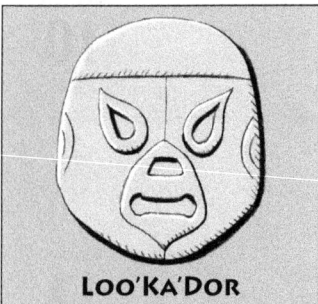

LOO'KA'DOR

Patron of mask-wearing Mayans afflicted with **Rez'el** mania.

72

monday

12

285

73

tuesday

13

284

Halley's Comet, 1759 — Giacomo Casanova, on his way to a tryst, looks up and exclaims, "Check out the tail on that!"

74

wednesday

14

283

75

thursday

15

282

Halley's Comet, 607— The Slavs, having recently invented the heavy plow, are so bushed they sleep right through it.

76

friday

16

281

77

saturday

17

280

St. Patrick's Day

78

sunday

18

279

Birthday of noted American psychic Edgar Cayce

MARCH

S	M	T	W	T	F	S
				1	2	3
4	5	6	7	8	9	10
11	12	13	14	15	16	17
18	19	20	21	22	23	24
25	26	27	28	29	30	31

...SIS BOOM B'OL!

Mural-size carvings along the back wall of the B'ol Hall of Fame commemorate centuries'-long city-state sports rivalries. Scholars now believe that the end of Mayan civilization was hastened by widespread rioting of jubilant Uxmal Monkey fans celebrating their home-team's first playoff victory in more than 400 years.

The only recorded instance of a B'ol double-header— with the second contest played as a torchlit night game — ended in tragedy (open flames + feathered headdresses = disaster). After that, games were played only in daylight and scheduled decades in advance to avoid eclipse-delays.

Buddha Claimant Ram Bahadur Bomjon, who disappeared on this date in 2006, is scheduled to return on this date in 2012. Leave a light on.

monday
19
278

80

Vernal Equinox
Memo: Congratulate Vern
Halley's Comet, 1066 — Marks William the Conqueror's victory at the Battle of Hastings. Better than fireworks, which don't exist.

tuesday
20
277

81

Zoroastrian New Year (Norouz)
Birthday of Russ Meyer

wednesday
21
276

82

Halley's Comet, 141 — Startled Chinese scholar spills ink on newly-invented paper, think it looks cool, invents calligraphy.

thursday
22
275

83

friday
23
274

84

saturday
24
273

85

sunday
25
272

MARCH

S	M	T	W	T	F	S
				1	2	3
4	5	6	7	8	9	10
11	12	13	14	15	16	17
18	19	20	21	22	23	24
25	26	27	28	29	30	31

Notes

THE FORTNIGHTLY GLYPH

WIZ'DOM

Symbol of the feared shaman **Den'tizt**
who could make grown Mayans weep.

86

monday
26
271

87

tuesday
27
270

88

wednesday
28
269

89

thursday
29
268

Birthday of Oscar Meyer

90

friday
30
267

91

saturday
31
266

92

April Fool's Day
Memo: Last one, be cruel.

sunday
1
265

MAYANOMICS

When it came to commerce, Mayans were shrewd, competitive and ruthless (records confirm there were no Mayans named "Ruth"). They lived by the law of supply and demand as well as the law of the jungle.

Referred to as the "Phoenicians of the Yucatan" by historians who know what that means, the Mayans, some experts believe, deliberately ended their calendar in 2012 to insure the need for a 2013 – 7139 edition.

Trades were conducted on the barter system or "rock, paper, scissors" until cocoa beans became standard currency throughout the empire in the late pre-classical era. Ceramic bowls engraved "Take a Bean, Leave a Bean" litter the site of Chichen Itza's enormous "Mall of Mesoamerica."

I'Ar'Es

Mayan city-states imposed hefty taxes on merchants, collecting them every Ides of April in an elaborate ceremony at the temple of the fearsome and vengeful god **I'Ar'Es**, who's motto was "In Guac We Trust". The disgruntled payees "spilled their beans" of cocoa which were then tallied up in increments equal to the weight of a human heart; a none-too-subtle reminder of the penalty for tax fraud. Late payments could also incur the wrath of the bean counters and result in painful "audits," wherein the offender tried to explain his negligence often without the benefit of his tongue.

TY'KOON

Ty'koon was a mythical trickster-demigod who routinely got away with short-changing I'Ar'Es. Known for his strange headdress, shiny pyramids and legions of apprentices, he was a folk hero to Mayan taxpayers. Some historians theorize Ty'koon may have been a merchant who lived in the early classical period, but most agree that his persona and exploits are too ridiculous to be true.

APRIL

S	M	T	W	T	F	S
1	2	3	4	5	6	7
8	9	10	11	12	13	14
15	16	17	18	19	20	21
22	23	24	25	26	27	28
29	30					

DIDN'T SEE THAT COMING

Recent findings suggest that it wasn't decades of drought and crop failures that sank the Mayan economy. Instead, visiting extraterrestrials convinced Mayan merchants to outsource their manufacturing to China, offering to transport the raw materials and return with finished goods. While it seemed like a good deal (their shipping and handling charges were quite reasonable), the aliens neglected to specify that when they said, "We'll swing by with your stuff the next time we're in the neighborhood," they meant, "In 13,000 earth years."

THIS WEEK IN MAYAN HISTORY

1517 Although gold was valuable to the Mayans, it wasn't nearly as precious as jade, salt, feathers or cocoa. When the Conquistadors showed up in search of gold and showed little interest in anything else, the Mayans misjudged them as none too bright and, therefore, probably not much of a threat.

93

monday

2

264

94

tuesday

3

263

95

wednesday

4

Birthday of Maya Angelou

262

96

thursday

5

261

97

friday

6

260

98

saturday

7

First Day of Passover

259

99

sunday

8

Easter Sunday

258

THE LEGEND OF P'NZI

P'Nzi, a successful merchant in no-one-knew-what,
sold shares in a new "state-of-the-art" ziggurat
to well-off Mayans in exchange for their finest goods.

The value of each share was inscribed on tablets made of
dried mud "dredged from the most sacred depths
of the Amazon". They sold like hot tacos.

The ziggurat, dedicated to the almighty god P'so rose on a
far-off hilltop stone by stone. The value of each share
also ascended, even more spectacularly.

Members of P'Nzi's cult, who later claimed he had
hypnotized them, peddled shares to a widening circle,
from B'ol team owners to warriors and court jesters.

One day a child ventured to the site of the ziggurat and
found it to be a single stack of stones piled high.
Angered investors vowed to sacrifice P'Nzi to P'so.

Unable to find his heart, they cut out his purse.
P'Nzi cultists, like Ma'Doff, learned their lesson —
a pyramid scheme doesn't need a pyramid.

APRIL

S	M	T	W	T	F	S
1	2	3	4	5	6	7
8	9	10	11	12	13	14
15	16	17	18	19	20	21
22	23	24	25	26	27	28
29	30					

EXTREMELY SHORT FORM

To accommodate end-timers Congress have amended the tax law and mandated the IRS to issue a form that is even eazier than the 1040EZ.

The 2012 1040EZX has merely three lines after Name, Address, and SSN:
1) Adjusted Gross Income
2) Total Payments and Credits
3) Amount We'll Never See

A signature is optional. It does allow the taxpayer to contribute $3 to The Rebuild the World Fund.

THE FORTNIGHTLY GLYPH

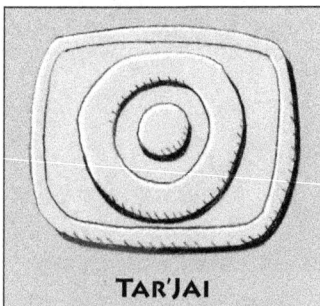

TAR'JAI

Avatar of the Mall of Mesoamerica's slightly more upscale big box store.

100

monday

9

257

101

tuesday

10

256

102

wednesday

11

255

103

thursday

12

254

104

friday

13

253

105

saturday

14

252

Last Day of Passover
Birthday of Erich Von Däniken,
visionary author of *Chariots of the Gods*

106

sunday

15

251

Eastern Orthodox Easter
RMS Titanic's 100th anniversary since the sinking in 1912,
which just might have inspired the IRS to establish Tax Day.

APRIL

S	M	T	W	T	F	S
	1	2	3	4	5	6	7
8	9	10	11	12	13	14
15	16	17	18	19	20	21
22	23	24	25	26	27	28
29	30					

ILL ALONG
THE WATCHTOWER

The Jehovah's Witness magazine *The Watchtower* quotes a pastor who claims that "Sometime between April 16 and 23, 1957, Armageddon will sweep the world! Millions of persons will perish in its flames and the land will be scorched." The magazine receives no Pulitzer nominations that year.

THE FORTNIGHTLY GLYPH

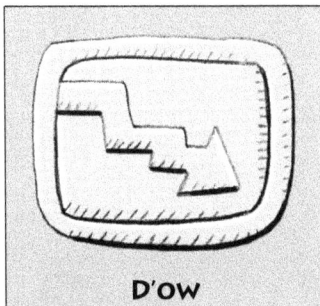

D'OW

The symbol of fickle fortune — for both Bulls and Bears.

107

monday
16
250

108

tuesday
17
249

109

Halley's Comet, 1145 — On the eve of The Second Crusade, reluctant French chevaliers are convinced it is a sign from God — to stay home.

wednesday
18
248

110

thursday
19
247

111

Halley's Comet, 295 — St. Nicholas is awestruck, and years later, when he moves to the North Pole, names one of his reindeer in its honor.
Halley's Comet, 1910 — The next day the report of Mark Twain's death was not in the least bit exaggerated.

friday
20
246

112

saturday
21
245

113

Earth Day
Memo: Recycle *this*, tree-hugger!

sunday
22
244

APRIL

S	M	T	W	T	F	S
1	2	3	4	5	6	7
8	9	10	11	12	13	14
15	16	17	18	19	20	21
22	23	24	25	26	27	28
29	30					

Notes

THE FORTNIGHTLY GLYPH

B'A C'OAD

ID symbol tattooed on slaves' scalps
to speed up check out at auctions.

114

monday

23

243

115

tuesday

24

242

116

wednesday

25

241

Birthday of Shirley MacLaine

117

thursday

26

240

118

friday

27

239

119

saturday

28

238

120

sunday

29

237

COME WHAT MAIZE

Much of modern Mexican cuisine originated with the Mayans — breakfast burritos, nacho platters, Crunchwrap Supreme® — but arguably the greatest of all Mayan culinary contributions is chocolate. Usually served as a spicy drink, chocolate was an important part of religious festivals and celebratory events.

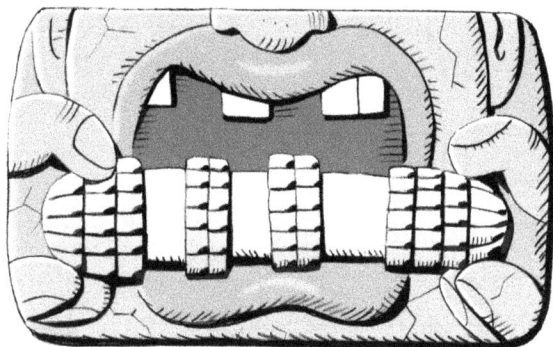

M'AAZ

The cocoa bean from which chocolate is made was worth far more than its weight in gold and, like a rich guy lighting cigars with $20 bills, wealthier Mayans enjoyed putting their money where there mouths were by popping them like so many peanuts.

Each region of the empire had its culinary specialties: coastal areas produced fish tacos, lowland farmers were masters of maize (which lent its name to the voracious demigod **M'Aaz**), and city dwellers lined up to be overcharged for "nouvelle Mayan" consisting of half an avocado, some chopped mango, a piece of fish the size of your thumbnail and a single cocoa bean for dessert.

One staple of the Mayan diet that thankfully didn't make it onto modern menus is canis domesticus, known in pre-Columbian Mesoamerica as "The other other white meat" or "Here, boy!"

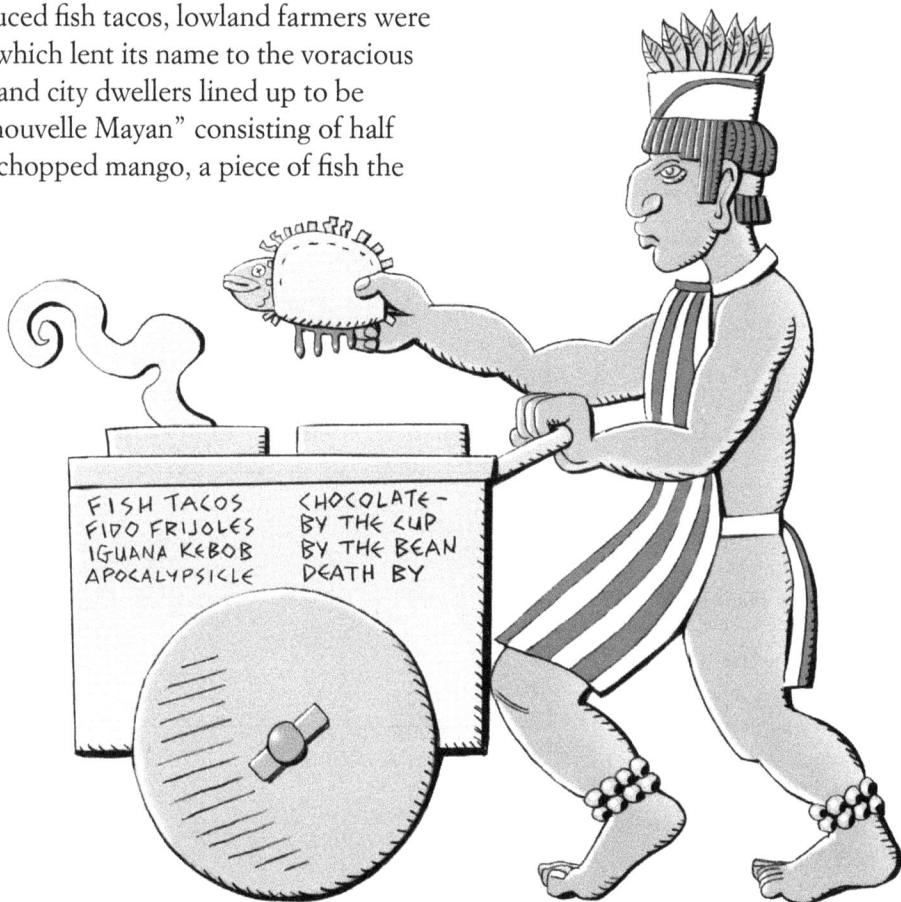

FISH TACOS
FIDO FRIJOLES
IGUANA KEBOB
APOCALYPSICLE

CHOCOLATE-
BY THE CUP
BY THE BEAN
DEATH BY

MAYAN STREET VENDOR

MAY

S	M	T	W	T	F	S
		1	2	4	4	5
6	7	8	9	10	11	12
13	14	15	16	17	18	19
20	21	22	23	24	25	26
27	28	29	30	31		

Notes

THIS WEEK IN MAYAN HISTORY

240 BCE The first "Cinco de Maya" feast is held during the earliest known appearance of Halley's Comet. Despite the comet's returning only every 75 years, the celebration becomes an annual event, mostly because of this one shaman's kickass margarita mix.

121

monday
30
236

122

tuesday
1
235

May Day
Memo: Mayday!

123

wednesday
2
234

124

thursday
3
233

125

friday
4
232

126

saturday
5
231

Cinco de Mayo
Memo: Mezcal!

127

sunday
6
230

MAY

S	M	T	W	T	F	S
		1	2	4	4	5
6	7	8	9	10	11	12
13	14	15	16	17	18	19
20	21	22	23	24	25	26
27	28	29	30	31		

THE GUACAMOLE CREATION MYTH

While bringing avocados to a feast, **Quetzalcoatl**, the feathered serpent god, bumps into **G'wok**, god of side dishes, who is bringing the salsa. They knock each other down, dropping everything.

G'wok: Hey! You got avocado on my minced red onion, serrano chiles, cilantro leaves, lemon or lime juice, salt, dash of black pepper and half-a-tomato!

Quetzalcoatl: Oh, yeah! You got minced red onion, serrano chiles, cilantro leaves, lemon or lime juice, salt, dash of black pepper and half-a-tomato on my smashed avocados!

G'wok: Hmmm, this tastes pretty good...

128

monday

7

229

129

tuesday

8

228

130

wednesday

9

227

131

thursday

10

226

132

friday

11

225

133

saturday

12

224

134

sunday

13

223

Mother's Day

Simple Gifts Mom Will Always Remember

Nothing touches Mom's heart on her special day like a gift you made with your own two hands. She brought you into this world, and, chances are, she'll be there when you go out in a few short months. Show her how much you care by taking a little extra time to make something personal.

We've got a few cute suggestions here, but feel free to use your imagination to tailor the gift to your Mom's personality. Don't worry about craftsmanship — her eyes aren't that good, anyway — it really is the thought that counts. And think of the money you'll save.

Pipe-cleaner and puff ball sculptures of
that lovable pest, the Bubonic plague-bearing flea.

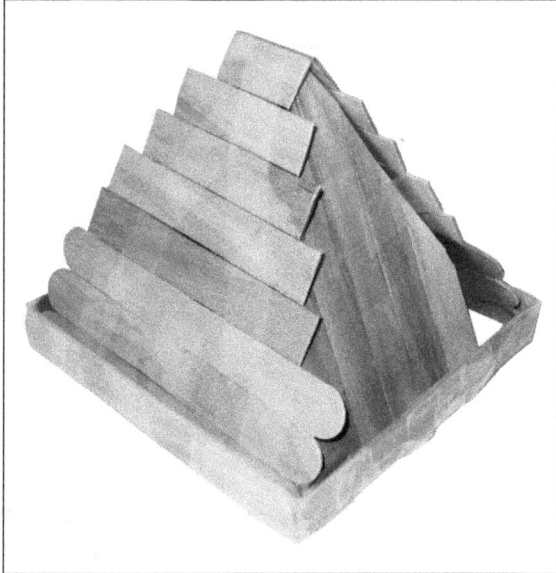

A pyramid hat made from ice cream sticks
to help her channel cosmic energy.

A doomsday clock decorated
with Smiley and Saddy Face buttons.

A hand-painted mug that celebrates the sacrifices
Mom has made for you.

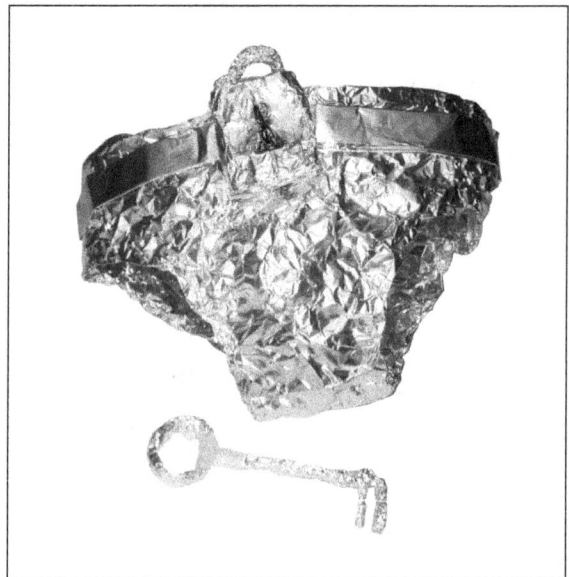

An aluminum-foil chastity belt to be used
in case of alien abduction.

MAY

COMETOSE

By the time Halley's Comet made its 1910 appearance and the earth passed through its tail on May 19th, science had replaced superstition as the basis for irrational fears about it. Having learned that: a) earth would pass through the comet's tail; and b) comet's tails are made up of dense clouds of dust and (yes, poisonous) gases, much of the public concluded that, "We're all gonna die!" and eagerly bought "comet pills" sold by wily entrepreneurs as protection from certain doom. In fact, the only recorded injuries were the bruises astronomers got from slapping their palms to their foreheads.

THE FORTNIGHTLY GLYPH

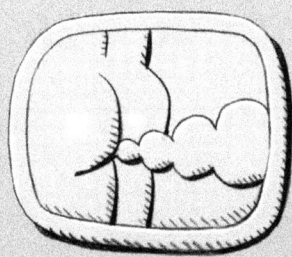

TA'KO

Patron of unwelcome dinner guests and namesake of a noxious volcano.

135

monday
14
222

136

tuesday
15
221

137

wednesday
16
220

138

thursday
17
219

Ascension Day
Memo: Get high.

139

friday
18
218

140

saturday
19
217

141

Annular Solar Eclipse — Do not stare directly into sun, but if you can't resist, first apply SPF 45 sunblock to your corneas.
French Presidential Election
Memo: Don't bet on Dominique Strauss-Kahn.
Halley's Comet, 760 — Provides fleeting night light in Dark Ages, but most of population is illiterate anyway.

sunday
20
216

MAY

S	M	T	W	T	F	S
		1	2	4	4	5
6	7	8	9	10	11	12
13	14	15	16	17	18	19
20	21	22	23	24	25	26
27	28	29	30	31		

HAROLD CAMPING'S TOP 10 EXCUSES FOR WHY THE WORLD DIDN'T END ON MAY 21, 2011:

10) Mayan restraining order prohibits end of world before December 21, 2012.

9) Overslept.

8) No, no, no, that's when *As the World Turns* ends.

7) It was supposed to be a surprise, but once word got out, God changed the date (he can do that, you know).

6) Really curious how they'll pull off Ashton Kutcher's replacing Charlie Sheen.

5) Just not feeling all that "raptury."

4) Haven't sold all of the "It's the End of the World and All I Got Was This Lousy T-Shirt" t-shirts, yet.

3) Couldn't find a sitter.

2) Wanted to see what kind of crazy stunt Donald Trump pulls next.

1) Traffic.

THE FORTNIGHTLY GLYPH

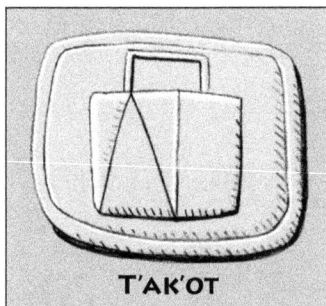

T'AK'OT

Prized talisman for the Mayan Missus, along with **Re'Heet** and **Pot'luk**.

142

monday
21
215

2011: The Rapture. Where were you when it didn't happen?

143

tuesday
22
214

144

wednesday
23
213

145

thursday
24
212

146

friday
25
211

Halley's Comet, 240 BCE — Dude, it totally blows their minds.

147

saturday
26
210

148

sunday
27
209

Pentecost
Shavout
Memo: Find out how you celebrate either one.

MAY

S	M	T	W	T	F	S
		1	2	4	4	5
6	7	8	9	10	11	12
13	14	15	16	17	18	19
20	21	22	23	24	25	26
27	28	29	30	31		

Notes

149

monday
28
208

Memorial Day

150

tuesday
29
207

151

wednesday
30
206

152

thursday
31
205

153

friday
1
204

154

saturday
2
203

155

sunday
3
202

MAYA OWN TRUE LOVE

When you think "Mayans" and "matters of the heart," romance probably isn't the first thing that pops into your head.

Mayans did, of course, fall in love and marry; not that the two things necessarily had much to do with each other. Marriages were arranged by the couple's parents with a professional matchmaker/wedding planner who would gauge their likely compatibility based on social rank, astrology, numerology and a hot-or-not scale from "A'oog'a!" to "Y'x!"

Unlike some pre-Columbian cultures (yeah, I'm looking at you Aztecs), Mayans didn't allow polygamy, but concubines were okay. Divorce was easy; brides came with a one-year satisfaction guarantee and were returnable so long as the groom's family had kept the receipt.

Some couplings were happier than others and the battle of the sexes was part of daily life. The newly discovered, *Men are from Baja, Women are from Acapulco*, an instructional pamphlet for Mayan youths approaching adulthood, advises that, "while single men may decorate themselves with paint, only married men are allowed tattoos because they are already accustomed to pain."

HER'PIIZ

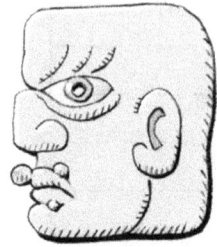

AL'MONI

KUK'OLD

EVIL MARRIAGE SPIRITS

MAA'TZ, TALISMAN OF THE SO-CALLED "SLINGSHOT" WEDDING

JUNE

S	M	T	W	T	F	S
					1	2
3	4	5	6	7	8	9
10	11	12	13	14	15	16
17	18	19	20	21	22	23
24	25	26	27	28	29	30

Notes

156

monday

4

201

157

tuesday

5

200

158

Second and last solar transit of the planet Venus of this century — Hopes not to get stuck in rush hour traffic.

2012 European Football Championship — Hosted by Poland and Ukraine. Bring your own scorecard.

wednesday

6

199

159

thursday

7

198

160

friday

8

197

161

Halley's Comet, 1456 — Pope Callixtus III excommunicates the comet as an instrument of the devil. The comet spins its head around 360° and hisses, "Your mother darns socks in Hell."

saturday

9

196

162

sunday

10

195

JUNE

TOP 10 FATHER'S DAY GIFT REQUESTS

10) Noose-quality flowered necktie.

9) Stiff-B-Gon Zombie repellent.

8) World's Best Dad life vest.

7) Duke Nukem post-postapocalyptic video game, *Duke Stonem*.

6) $50 gift certificate from Survival Sam's.

5) Sharper Image Wheezalizer volcanic ash filter.

4) Casual hazmat suit from Men's Wearhouse.

3) Deluxe Hammacher-Schlemmer Geiger counter with portable emergency light.

2) Strontium-90 BBQ Grill Master 4-piece set.

1) Happy ending massage.

THE FORTNIGHTLY GLYPH

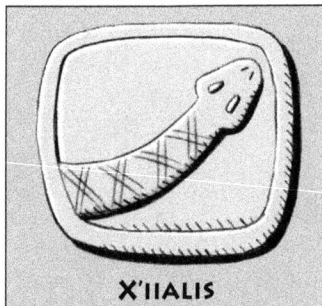

X'IIALIS

Trademark for shamans' miracle elixir said to cure "the pooped python."

163

monday
11
194

164

tuesday
12
193

165

wednesday
13
192

166

thursday
14
191

Flag Day
Memo: A white one would be appropriate.

167

friday
15
190

168

saturday
16
189

169

sunday
17
188

Father's Day

the Mystickal Jüweler

Let us blow your mind
like we blow our glass!

Satanic Nose Rings!
"Twilight" Blood Vials!
Day of the Dead Anklets!
Milagro Phallus Bracelets!
Impurity Rings!
Ears pierced before your eyes!

666 Warlock Way • Taos NM

TRY A DRIVE-BY NOSTRADAMUS BUS TOUR

Climax Adventures Ltd. and **Sveiki, Latvia!** invite you to explore the amazing prophecies of Nostradamus as they might apply to the history of scenic Latvia.

The *Drive-By Nostradamus Bus Tour* will whisk you in climate-controlled luxury from Riga to Ventspils to Daugavpils as your college-educated guide explains how the 16th-century seer's visions changed the world. And maybe even Latvia. We predict you'll love it! Call 888-CLI-MAXX or visit climaxadventures.com.

From **$179***

* Does not include airfare, dinner, commemorative plasticware, inflatable neck rests, antidiarrhetics, potable water, compasses, or "complimentary" snacks.

Climax Adventures Ltd.
c o m e   w i t h   u s

"Hasta la Vista, Baby?"

Let world-renowned post-apocalyptic expert Dr. El Bondigas prepare you and yours for the Aftermath. Are there hidden fees? Will it be pet-friendly? Is plastic accepted? Will you need a jacket? Get answers to these and all your questions about the days after tomorrow.

Dr. El Bondigas, BA, SOB

Consultation by Appointment Only
Dial 1-877-END-TIME

Indulge Yourself Like There's
No Tomorrow with a Decadent

FUBAR

Rich, Dark Chocolate on the Outside
All Kinds of Weird Sh*t on the Inside

**You'll be
Filled Up Beyond All Reason**

Sybill's Sweet Shoppe ★ Milky Way, ME

Draw Me
Win a $200 Art Course

Send us your drawing of Grimmy done in any medium (excluding bodily fluids) and our panel of experts will decide if you qualify for a $200 Art Course (2 sessions) or if you need the full course and must pay $1200. Then receive lessons from some of the most famous artists from the Beyond including Rembrant, Picasso & Smith right at home. Mail your artwork with $50 and a SASE to:

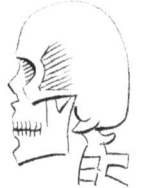

**The Famous Dead Artists School
Pine Office Box 13
Elysian Fields, TX 75642**

Can't Afford a Beach Vacation This Summer?
Want Your Kids Ready for the Coming Flood?
Here's Good Clean Fun That's Wet and Wild!

CAMP SAC XIB CHAC

Named for the Mayan God of the White North Rain, this glistening jewel of a sleepaway camp sits nestled in Washington State's majestic Hoh Rain Forest. Here spruce trees soar to heights of more than 200 feet. Here big-leaf maples are so densely covered with mosses that they look like shaggy mastodons. Here your socks never dry.

Dewy-faced kids, ages 6 to 16, experience sand-bagging, ark building, life-rafting, and swimming, swimming, and more swimming. Global Warming never felt so warm. Or fuzzy.
Call 1(867) WET-GEAR or visit moldandmildew/camp.biz.

CAMP
SAC
XIB
CHAC
SOAK IT IN

From **$20.12***

* Per camper per day. Does not include PVC rain suits, umbrellas, water wings, talc, anti-fungal sprays, inhalers, dry sheets, or hair driers.

Only $5 for Your First Session

**The Exercise Sensation
Sweeping Lynchburg VA!**

RAPTURECIZE

Shape Up for the Final Judgment
Sweatin' to the Scriptures!

Call 877-ALL-ELUIA

With coupon only. Kneeling pad not included.

2nd Scoop Free Ice Floe Float

Delicious Flavors:
Root Berg!
CO_2 Cola!
Minty Melt!
Cherry Glacier!
Always made
with real
Antarctic Ice!

Tasti-Melt Freeze Treats • Cold Harbor VA
With coupon only. Not responsible for cracked teeth.

$15⁰⁰ OFF
One Way Ticket

FINAL SUNSET CRUISE
Sail to the Bottom of the Sea in Luxury

Slip 7, Hemingway Marina • Suicide Key, FL

With coupon only. Boat leaves at dusk on the 21st of each month through December. Does not return.

JUNE

S	M	T	W	T	F	S
					1	2
3	4	5	6	7	8	9
10	11	12	13	14	15	16
17	18	19	20	21	22	23
24	25	26	27	28	29	30

NOBLE NUPTIALS

On the occasion of a royal wedding, the Mayan scribe caste would reliably go into full swoon and commence gushing and squealing with delight over every detail about the happy couple, the guest list, who wore what and how tasty the chupacabra kabab at the reception was. In short, they got busy seriously kissing aristocratic ass. Unseemly? Maybe, but staying on the good side of anyone related to the guy who "randomly" picked the next human sacrifice wasn't a bad survival strategy.

170

monday
18
187

171

tuesday
19
186

172

wednesday
20
185

Summer Solstice
Memo: Goes great with chips.

173

thursday
21
184

174

friday
22
183

175

saturday
23
182

176

sunday
24
181

JUNE

S	M	T	W	T	F	S
					1	2
3	4	5	6	7	8	9
10	11	12	13	14	15	16
17	18	19	20	21	22	23
24	25	26	27	28	29	30

Notes

THE FORTNIGHTLY GLYPH

B'RIIF

One of three mail fertility talismans
along with **Box'a** and **K'man'do**.

177

monday
25
180

178

tuesday
26
179

179

wednesday
27
178

180

Halley's Comet, 451 — Attila the Hun sees it as an omen of his conquest of the Goths, although he expects less luck with the Emos.

thursday
28
177

181

friday
29
176

182

saturday
30
175

183

Presidential Elections in Mexico — National Action Party's new slogan: Drugs or Bust.

sunday
1
174

CRYSTAL BALLS

While the Mayans didn't predict three-day weekends and backyard barbecues, they did make several forecasts regarding a "...great empire that will rise in the North" that seem to have our name on them. Here are the top ten:

10) A new tribe will be formed by men with removable white hair; one of them will have four eyes and control fire in the sky.

9) They will eat anything that's on a stick and, if you put chocolate on it, they will eat the stick.

8) Their mountains will be purple.

Q'BUUM
The Spaniards introduced gunpowder at Dependence Day celebrations which marked their conquest of the Mayans.

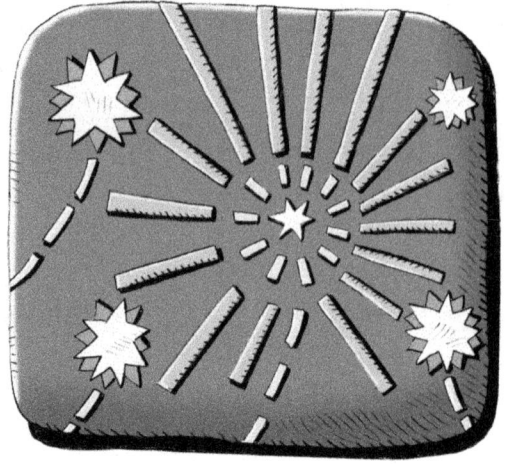

W'AN, Q'BUUM'S 1ST CASUALTY

7) Voices will float on the wind: pictures, too, but not in color until the 1960s.

6) They will eagerly lose their money to our descendants in games of chance.

5) You think our rulers are weird, wait till you see what this bunch coughs up.

4) They will travel to the moon, but then come right back.

3) They will be a good and decent people who will kick the asses of anyone who says that they aren't.

2) Their medicine men will have powerful magic; side effects may include, headache, dry mouth, nausea, dizziness upon standing, constipation, thoughts of suicide and/or erections lasting more than four hours.

1) Will believe that neither death nor taxes are unavoidable.

JULY

S	M	T	W	T	F	S
1	2	3	4	5	6	7
8	9	10	11	12	13	14
15	16	17	18	19	20	21
22	23	24	25	26	27	28
29	30	31				

SUMMER MORE ACCURATE THAN OTHERS

July 1999 was Nostradamus's pick in the Armageddon arrival date-sweepstakes; and of course you remember what happened in 7/99 (hint: nothing). His reputation as a foreteller of the future owes more to the wishful thinking of his interpreters than anything in his poetical prognostications. Also keep in mind when trying to decipher his enigmatic quatrains that Nostradamus's day job was as an apothecary (pharmacist) and just maybe he was helping himself to free samples of the strong stuff.

Nostradamus brews up his heady Elixir of Posterity.

184

monday
2
173

Nostradamus dies on this date in 1566; whether he saw it coming or not has been the source of many boring arguments.

185

tuesday
3
172

186

wednesday
4
171

Independence Day
Birthday of Meyer Lansky

187

thursday
5
170

188

friday
6
169

189

saturday
7
168

190

sunday
8
167

JULY

S	M	T	W	T	F	S
1	2	3	4	5	6	7
8	9	10	11	12	13	14
15	16	17	18	19	20	21
22	23	24	25	26	27	28
29	30	31				

Notes

THE FORTNIGHTLY GLYPH

L'VIZ

Wildly popular idol who's name
meant "He who's pelvis quakes."

191

monday

9

166

192

tuesday

10

165

193

wednesday

11

164

194

thursday

12

163

195

friday

13

162

196

saturday

14

161

197

sunday

15

160

DEGRADING ON THE CURVE

Although still unauthenticated by experts and currently for sale on eBay, this 16th century drawing is believed to be of a Mayan wall-carving (since destroyed) that envisions the future map of North America.

Note how the numbers' spiraling outward echoes the Greeks' ideal geometric proportions (the "Golden Ratio"), and how their locations coincide with the sites of major U.S. cities. This, combined with the eerily on-target text describing each (translated below) exhibits, yet again, the Mayans' astounding prescience. Unless it doesn't.

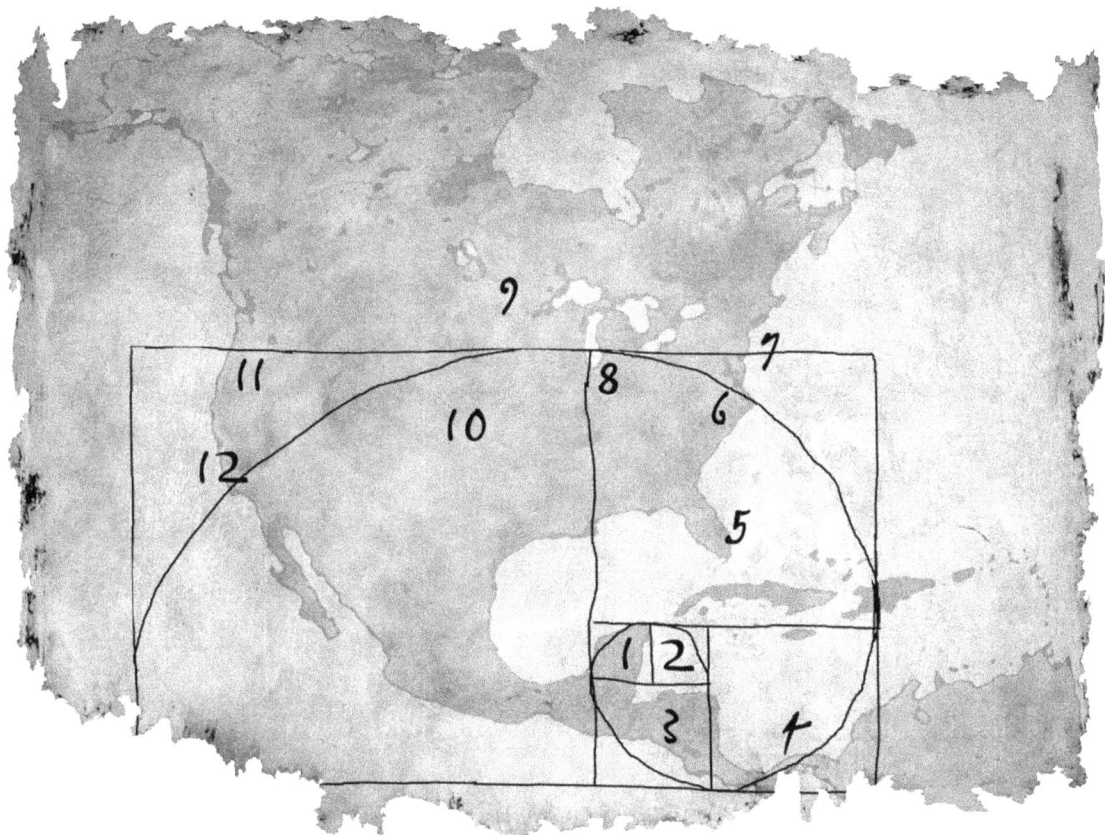

1) "The Big Avocado." If You Can Make it *Here*, You Can Make it *Anywhere*! (offer expires 12/21/2012).

2) View from beach front timeshare we just bought.

3) It's not nicknamed "The Mosquito Coast" for nothing.

4) Good spot for moat to keep out the Incas.

5) That explorers seek the fountain of youth here will turn out to be deeply ironic.

6) Once a swamp, always a swamp.

7) City of great pyramids that reach the sky and have rents to match.

8) Their dogs and winds will both be chilly.

9) Free health care.

10) Fruited plains over which many will fly, but few will land.

11) Too rainy here to see anything clearly, much less the future.

12) Gateway between this world and the world of dreams; traffic will be a nightmare.

JULY

S	M	T	W	T	F	S
1	2	3	4	5	6	7
8	9	10	11	12	13	14
15	16	17	18	19	20	21
22	23	24	25	26	27	28
29	30	31				

THIS WEEK IN MAYAN HISTORY

289 BCE The first recorded visit by extraterrestrials occurs when the parents of some juvenile delinquent aliens land to apologize for their offsprings' crop circle vandalism, abductions and anal probing. They assure the Mayans that the miscreants have been grounded for the next 50,000 light years. "Kids," they shrug, "Whaddaya gonna do?"

198

monday
16
159

199

tuesday
17
158

200

Halley's Comet, 912 — Byzantine Emperor Alexander hopes that his spotting of the comet will get someone to call him Great.

wednesday
18
157

201

thursday
19
156

202

Ramadan Begins

friday
20
155

203

saturday
21
154

204

sunday
22
153

JULY

S	M	T	W	T	F	S
1	2	3	4	5	6	7
8	9	10	11	12	13	14
15	16	17	18	19	20	21
22	23	24	25	26	27	28
29	30	31				

Notes

THE FORTNIGHTLY GLYPH

D'OOD

Secret greeting translated as,
"Are you also a man with no shame?"

205

monday
23
152

206

tuesday
24
151

207

wednesday
25
150

208

thursday
26
149

209

Opening Ceremony of the 2012 Summer Olympics in London —
Can't wait for the high dive off the London Eye into the Thames.
Birthday of Maya Rudolph

friday
27
148

210

saturday
28
147

211

Tisha B'Av
Memo: Is she that Israeli supermodel?

sunday
29
146

AUGUST

THE HUMID CONDITION

When the dog days of August rolled into the Yucatan, any metropolitan Mayans who could, showed up on the doorstep of their closest relative whose beachfront ziggurat had a spare room with cross-ventilation.

At the same time, all of the city's shamans would also take off for parts unknown, leaving the more neurotic Mayans to ponder the meaningless of existence on their own for several

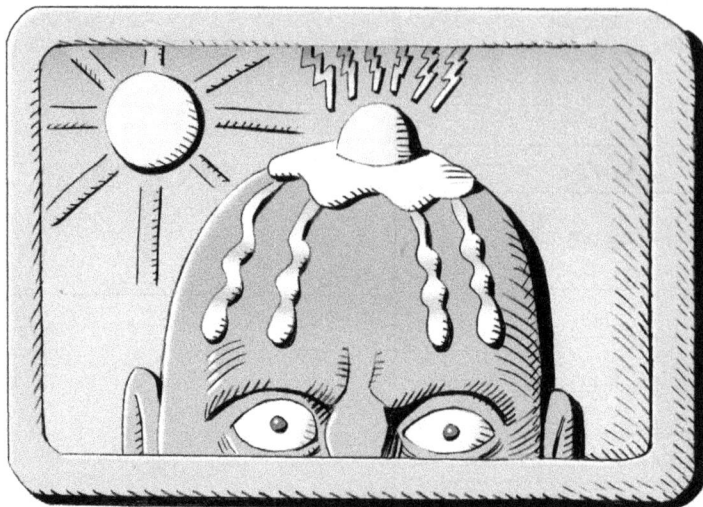

S'HVTZ, HOT-HEADED SUMMER SPIRIT

sweltering weeks. Where the shamans went each August was a mystery until the recent discovery of carvings that depict groups of them partying like it's 2011.

For the workaday every-Mayan, however, this season just meant more of the same old same old, only with more sweating. The closest they got to even a "working vacation" was short-term conscription into the army. While these military stints were usually just for quick village raid or two, such "vacations" sometimes became permanent.

VACATIONERS AT K'LB M'ED IN A'KA'PUL'KO

AUGUST

S	M	T	W	T	F	S
			1	2	3	4
5	6	7	8	9	10	11
12	13	14	15	16	17	18
19	20	21	22	23	24	25
26	27	28	29	30	31	

THE WASH B'OL

Rain delays frequently interrupted August B'ol games and players returning to the muddy fields were often swallowed up whole into the deep, waterlogged muck, forcing the middle relievers to come in early and sometimes clearing the bench.

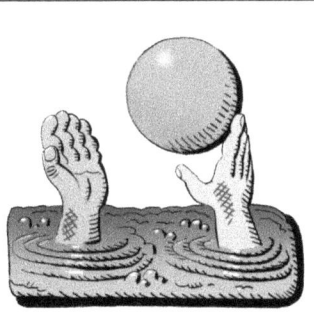

Climactic moment in the storied 201 finals as X'ac attempts a pass to Ko'B under adverse playing conditions.

212

monday
30
145

213

tuesday
31
144

214

wednesday
1
143

215

thursday
2
142

216

friday
3
141

217

saturday
4
140

218

sunday
5
139

AUGUST

S	M	T	W	T	F	S
			1	2	3	4
5	6	7	8	9	10	11
12	13	14	15	16	17	18
19	20	21	22	23	24	25
26	27	28	29	30	31	

Notes

THE FORTNIGHTLY GLYPH

N'OOKZ

Talismanic shield against the summer heat. Did squat against the humidity.

219

monday

6

138

Halley's Comet, 87 BCE — Armenian King Tigranes II strikes coin with image of a star with a tail that bears a startling resemblance to Benji.

220

tuesday

7

137

221

wednesday

8

136

222

thursday

9

135

223

friday

10

134

224

saturday

11

133

225

sunday

12

132

Closing Ceremony of the 2012 Summer Olympics in London — One can only hope it includes Elton John and the other Queen being set upon by Wenlock, the one-eyed mascot.

DOOMSDAY FUNNIES

ZOMBIE

A.D.

XICC'I

GLOOMY TUNES

AUGUST

S	M	T	W	T	F	S
			1	2	3	4
5	6	7	8	9	10	11
12	13	14	15	16	17	18
19	20	21	22	23	24	25
26	27	28	29	30	31	

DOOMSDATES OF FUTURE PASSED

Best remembered for his role in Ed Wood's *Plan 9 From Outer Space*, The Amazing Criswell predicted that on August 18, 1999, a death ray from space would strike Denver, Colorado, turning metal into rubber. This would somehow lead to the collapse of civilization, widespread cannibalism and the end of the world. He also foretold that at this time Mae West (at the age of 106) would be president of the United States and that she, Criswell and Liberace's brother George would escape the impending carnage in a rocket ship to the moon. He didn't say what would happen once they got there, but it can't have been pretty.

Criswell later revised his end-of-the-word date to — you guessed it — December 21, 2012, and then fact check-proofed himself by dying in 1982.

226

monday
13
131

227

tuesday
14
130

228

wednesday
15
129

229

thursday
16
128

230

friday
17
127

231

saturday
18
126

232

sunday
19
125

S	M	T	W	T	F	S
			1	2	3	4
5	6	7	8	9	10	11
12	13	14	15	16	17	18
19	20	21	22	23	24	25
26	27	28	29	30	31	

Notes

THE FORTNIGHTLY GLYPH

P'ONG

A game young men were encouraged to play as a substitute for self-abuse.

233

monday
20
124

234

tuesday
21
123

235

wednesday
22
122

236

thursday
23
121

237

friday
24
120

238

saturday
25
119

239

Halley's Comet, 1531 — Francisco Pizarro conquers Incas in Peru — Mayans offer prayers to their petty demi-god S'ha'Den Froi'De.

sunday
26
118

September

Know Mas

Education for the average Mayan boy consisted of a couple of hours of instruction on the bow and arrow, and being thrown into a piranha-infested lake to learn how to swim. The Mayan male of means, however, was expected to expand his mind and financial prospects under expert tutelage. Females, regardless of class, were largely expected to stay at home and learn the rudiments of sewing, cooking and "smoking the pink pipe" from their mothers.

Primary schooling began at age three with toy ziggurats built from L'Go dried-dung blocks and games of play human sacrifice. In secondary school a youngster might begin his apprenticeship as an avocado merchant, a coffee farmer or a barista.

D'unz, Patron of Slow Learners

At institutions of higher learning like B'u and U'z El'ai, basket-weaving, ironically, was as prestigious a pursuit as cocoanomics. Body-piercing was considered a gut course. Many a Mayan mother wanted her son to attend medicinal herbs school, even as she wished her daughter would marry a shaman with a steady practice.

Top Students from the Maya High Yearblock

Z'itz
Uncomely girl voted most popular due to acrobatic chant-leading and love-making

K'illa
Captain of the B'ol Team who tore his own heart out after winning the championship

Ga'dar
aka He Who Loves Feathers, member of Thespians, Glee Club, Chocolateers and Cult of L'iza

In the waning years of the Empire, when young people had succumbed to indolence and the chewing of psychotropic roots, some venerable institutions tried to attract adult students by offering courses of dubious merit.

Some of these classes, held under the cover of night, included *Is Quetzalcoatl Dead?*, *The Chocolate Orgasm*, and *Predict the End of the World and Get Rich*.

September

S	M	T	W	T	F	S
						1
2	3	4	5	6	7	8
9	10	11	12	13	14	15
16	17	18	19	20	21	22
23	24	25	26	27	28	29
30						

Notes

240

monday
27
117

241

tuesday
28
116

242

wednesday
29
115

243

thursday
30
114

244

friday
31
113

245

saturday
1
112

246

sunday
2
111

September

S	M	T	W	T	F	S
						1
2	3	4	5	6	7	8
9	10	11	12	13	14	15
16	17	18	19	20	21	22
23	24	25	26	27	28	29
30						

Notes

THE FORTNIGHTLY GLYPH

T'WIIT

Avian avatar of meaningless blather
— cousin to **B'lch**, **F'rt** & **T'xt**.

247

monday

3
110

Labor Day
Memo: Make it work.

101

tuesday

4
109

248

wednesday

5
108

Halley's Comet, 989 — The Chinese copy the comet's form for the
double-twist, long-tailed dumpling popular during the Song Dynasty.

249

thursday

6
107

250

friday

7
106

251

saturday

8
105

252

sunday

9
104

September

This rare piece of black slate etched with a Mayan student's lesson in hieroglyphic syllables belies a lack of respect for a substitute teacher.

The symbols correspond to those codified by Bishop Diego de Landa, the 16th-century Spaniard who imposed the Inquisition in the Yucatan, torturing innocents and destroying invaluable documents. He also produced a seminal study of the religion he set out to eradicate, and this less-than-accurate 27-character "alphabet."

253

monday
10
103

254

tuesday
11
102

255

wednesday
12
101

256

thursday
13
100

257

friday
14
99

258

Halley's Comet, 1682 — Edmond Halley sees namesake comet and plots its 75-76 year orbit which is confirmed in 1785, 42 years after his death. 271 years later Bill Haley & His Comets have a #1 hit with *Rock Around the Clock*. Eerie, hunh?

saturday
15
98

259

sunday
16
97

SEPTEMBER

S	M	T	W	T	F	S
						1
2	3	4	5	6	7	8
9	10	11	12	13	14	15
16	17	18	19	20	21	22
23	24	25	26	27	28	29
30						

Notes

THE FORTNIGHTLY GLYPH

RIT'LIN

Hyperactive young sprite too fond of
chocolate, coffee and coca.

260

monday
17
96

Rosh Ha Shanah
Memo: *This* is a New Year?

261

tuesday
18
95

262

wednesday
19
94

263

thursday
20
93

264

friday
21
92

265

saturday
22
91

Autumnal Equinox
Memo: The Fall of Man.

266

sunday
23
90

September

267

monday

24

89

268

tuesday

25

88

269

wednesday

26

87

Yom Kippur
Memo: You better atone but good!

270

thursday

27

86

Halley's Comet, 530 — After composing an impromptu free form poem in praise of the celestial phenomenon while accompanying himself on a hand drum, Pope Felix IV is dubbed The Cat.

271

Native American Day
Memo: Send Mayans note reading "I feels ya."

Halley's Comet, 1222 — Japanese storytellers weave the tale of the giant, fire-breathing Hallzilla created in the comet's glow who destroys Kamakura, seat of the Shogunate.

friday

28

85

272

saturday

29

84

273

sunday

30

83

THIS WEEK IN MAYAN HISTORY

862 A.D. When a band of Vikings lands in the Yucatan, some quick-thinking Mayans sell them beach front time-shares in Cancun. After extracting a hefty "security deposit" from the gullible Nordic knuckleheads, they point them back to Scandinavia via a "shortcut" that will take them directly through the Bermuda Triangle.

DAY OF THE REALLY MOST SINCERELY DEAD

The Mayans weren't so much interested in honoring the dead as making sure there were plenty of them.

Still, as indifferent as they were to the deaths of their enemies, their subjects and, well, pretty much everyone else, Mayan nobility spent years and fortunes erecting grandiose post-mortem monuments to their own fabulousness. Intent on "taking it with them," they planned to entomb not only themselves, but as many of their valuables as they could cram in there.

TRICKSTER B'ONZ ENTERTAINED CHILDREN AT BIRTHDAY PARTIES AND SKULL ROLLS

In the declining years of the Mayan empire, raiding treasure-filled royal tombs became common practice and was jokingly known as the "death tax." Unscrupulous tomb contractors built in hidden doorways which, when tapped on in just the right spot, opened secret passageways into the crypt for easier extraction of the goodies within. Some scholars believe this to be the origins of the modern piñata.

J'ZON

J'RII

B'O'Tx

HORRIFYING CEREMONIAL DAY OF THE DEAD MASKS

OCTOBER

A MAIZE & GRACE

October was also the time to harvest maize, mainstay of the Mayan diet. A good crop was cause for celebration. Feasts were had and offerings were made to the maize goddess; followed a few weeks later by exasperated whines of "maize for dinner again!?"

Mayans called their precious maize "Harvest Gold" and it (along with avocados) was the foundation of Mayan cuisine. Any well-stocked Mayan kitchen pantry was, therefore, aglow in Harvest Gold and avocado green.

Harvest time manifestation of demi-god M'Aaz set upon by his natural enemy, the diminutive Mexican Crow (*Corvus imparatus*).

274

monday

1

82

First Day of Sukkot

275

tuesday

2

81

Halley's Comet, 684 — The Nuremberg Chronicle, one of the earliest printed books, alludes to "a hairy star." Is it a reference to the comet or Alec Baldwin?

276

wednesday

3

80

277

thursday

4

79

278

friday

5

78

Birthday of Maya Lin

279

saturday

6

77

280

sunday

7

76

Last Day of Sukkot

OCTOBER

S	M	T	W	T	F	S
	1	2	3	4	5	6
7	8	9	10	11	12	13
14	15	16	17	18	19	20
21	22	23	24	25	26	27
28	29	30	31			

monday

Columbus Day

8
75

282

tuesday

Simhat Torah

9
74

GOODBYE COLUMBUS

On one of his return voyages to the New World and possibly after either some really bad grog or really good ganja, Christopher Columbus wrote a book of prophecies that penciled in Judgment Day for no later than 1656.

283

Halley's Comet, 12 BCE — Caesar Augustus, first emperor of the Roman Empire, commands that it appear again next week at his Ides of October Orgy.

wednesday

10
73

284

thursday

11
72

WHISENAUT WANT NOT

In his book *88 Reasons Why the Rapture will Occur in 1988*, Edgar Whisenaut, a former NASA engineer, warns mankind that The End will come on October 11 of the titular year. His book sells over 4 million copies, but sales fall off dramatically after October 12.

285

friday

12
71

286

saturday

13
70

THE FORTNIGHTLY GLYPH

OM'BRAAZ

Icon marked spot where warriors "drained the feathered serpent."

287

sunday

14
69

OCTOBER

HAROLD CAMPING'S TOP 10 EXCUSES FOR WHY THE WORLD DIDN'T END ON OCTOBER 21, 2011:

10) Overslept. Again. Note to self: get better alarm clock.

9) Hadn't finished packing.

8) The Lord-God Jehovah, wants me to see the next season of *Mad Men*.

7) I'm just really bad at math.

6) No, I mean really, really bad at math.

5) Maybe I changed my mind, okay? Yeah, maybe I can do that. World ends/World doesn't end. Maybe it's my call. Suck on it.

4) Wait, you thought I meant THIS October 21?

3) Still figuring out how to change Facebook status to "Raptured."

2) How do you know it didn't?

1) Psych!

288

monday
15
68

289

tuesday
16
67

290

wednesday
17
66

291

thursday
18
65

292

friday
19
64

293

saturday
20
63

294

Radio preacher Harold Camping's revised date for the end of the world (see May 21). And this time, he means it. For sure. Really.

sunday
21
62

RARE STONE-CUT PERIODICAL DEPICTING LEGENDARY DANDY U'STIZ T'ILLI STUDYING AN AVATAR OF KUKULCAN

October

S	M	T	W	T	F	S
	1	2	3	4	5	6
7	8	9	10	11	12	13
14	15	16	17	18	19	20
21	22	23	24	25	26	27
28	29	30	31			

COTTON PICKIN'

Having rid Salem, Massachusetts of its troublesome witches, Judge Cotton Mather deduced that the Second Coming would be in 1697. Upon the safe arrival of the year 1698, he recalculated it for 1716. In 1717, he checked his numbers again and reset the final countdown for 1736, but died eight years before that, leaving no instructions about what to do in the event of 1737.

THE FORTNIGHTLY GLYPH

M'OO'HER'Z

Icon marked spot where women gathered to "squat and squawk".

295

monday
22
61

296

tuesday
23
60

297

wednesday
24
59

298

Halley's Comet, 1301 — Dante Alighieri begins work on an epic narrative poem that describes an asteroid the size of Florence hurtling towards the Earth and the team of alchemists racing to stop it. He is exiled and never finishes it.

thursday
25
58

299

friday
26
57

300

Halley's Comet, 1607 — Settlers in Jamestown, Virginia, wonder if it is a heavenly sign from their Divine Maker or an hallucination caused by hunger.

saturday
27
56

301

sunday
28
55

November

Vie Oh Vie

Despite the autocratic nature of the Mayan Empire there were quasi-political campaigns for municipal underlings eager to serve at the whim of each city-state's monarch. Such hopefuls would mount months-long charm offensives designed to tickle those royal fancies. Their efforts culminated in November's Erection Day, when the aspirants put up huge, shaft-like shrines dedicated to their prospective patron in the city square.

Once all of the towers stood proudly upright, the candidates mounted platforms to have their bodies smeared with wild boar grease, and then commenced shinnying up the poles in a race to the empurpled knobs that crowned them.

The assembled royal family would encourage the climbers to alternately grunt like pigs and shout out well-worn slogans to the gathered throngs. Favored sentiments included a pledge to raise taxes, a condemnation of poison arrow control, and support for the death-and-dismemberment penalty. Each contestant was allowed to fling mud or any available bodily excretions at foes in an effort to slow their progress.

The first to sit astride the shrine's helmet-like apex was designated Vice Toady. Second place finisher was named Lickspittle-in-Chief, and the third, Court Jester. From the remaining losers, one was chosen randomly to serve as Ambassador to the Incas, and the rest were quartered and fed to the royal jaguars.

**S'Hmooz,
Patron of Mayan Politicians**

**Defaced Glyph of Candidate
1st Negative Campaign Slab**

NOVEMBER

S	M	T	W	T	F	S
				1	2	3
4	5	6	7	8	9	10
11	12	13	14	15	16	17
18	19	20	21	22	23	24
25	26	27	28	29	30	

Notes

monday
29
54

303

tuesday
30
53

304

wednesday
31
52

Halloween
Memo: Give all the little buggers raisins.

305

thursday
1
51

306

friday
2
50

307

saturday
3
49

308

sunday
4
48

End of Daylight Savings Time
Memo: Fall back, to your bomb shelter.

THE FORTNIGHTLY GLYPH

M'BII'N

Demigod who enchanted sleepers to
shuffle about and stuff there faces.

NOVEMBER

S	M	T	W	T	F	S
				1	2	3
4	5	6	7	8	9	10
11	12	13	14	15	16	17
18	19	20	21	22	23	24
25	26	27	28	29	30	

D'OH²

Not all Mayans bought into the infallibility of the Long Count calendar. In the 6th century AD, a cult developed around the belief that doomsday would arrive on December 21 of some year ending in "12" just not necessarily 2012. Called "Dodos" (short for "Dodecaphobia," fear of the number 12), they argued endlessly over which century's Year 12 would be the Big One, with 1212 a clear favorite.

Already a pretty skittish bunch, as 12/21/1212 approached, Dodos saw everything from a hangnail to a hurricane as evidence of impending doom. On the evening of December 20th, 1212, about half of the group dropped dead of fright; the other half dying of embarrassment on December 22nd. Their credibility and members gone, the Dodos were quickly forgotten.

Ironically, the Dodos' paranoia could have been useful when the Mayans encountered their first Europeans, a group of shipwrecked Spaniards, who washed up on the Yucatan shore. . . in 1511.

309

monday

5

47

310

tuesday

6

46

U.S. Presidential Election Day
Memo: Look for the Anti-Christ on ballot.

311

wednesday

7

45

312

thursday

8

44

313

friday

9

43

314

saturday

10

42

Halley's Comet, 1378 — Dmitri Donskoi of Moscow resists the Mongol Blue Horde, but it takes all his will power.

315

sunday

11

41

Veterans' Day

NOVEMBER

S	M	T	W	T	F	S
				1	2	3
4	5	6	7	8	9	10
11	12	13	14	15	16	17
18	19	20	21	22	23	24
25	26	27	28	29	30	

Notes

THE FORTNIGHTLY GLYPH

B'OOBZ

Fertility symbol, sister to **N'obz**,
Ba'Zoomz, and **Ga'Zon'Gaz**.

316

monday
12
40

Halley's Comet, 164 BCE — Lucius Aemilius Paullus Macedonicus is elected censor in Rome. Bans "chasing tail" jokes.

317

tuesday
13
39

Total Solar Eclipse — Visible in the South Pacific, even to the lei man.

318

wednesday
14
38

319

thursday
15
37

320

friday
16
36

Halley's Comet, 1835 — Of his birth, Mark Twain wrote, "I came in with Halley's Comet in 1835. It is coming again next year (1910), and I expect to go out with it." There is no record that they dated.

321

saturday
17
34

322

sunday
18
33

November

S	M	T	W	T	F	S
				1	2	3
4	5	6	7	8	9	10
11	12	13	14	15	16	17
18	19	20	21	22	23	24
25	26	27	28	29	30	

The Mayans domesticated the turkey (*Meleagris gallapavo*) 1,500 years before their northern cousins, the Wampanoag Indians, offered him to the Pilgrims for Thanksgiving dinner in 1621.

Although Mayan cooks never tried anything quite as ill-advised as a turducken (a turkey stuffed with a duck that's been stuffed with a chicken), recently discovered records show that for several decades in the 3rd century AD they experimented with deep-frying anything and everything.

The image above, for which there is no surviving explanatory text, leaves us to guess whether it is a public service announcement about the dangers of deep-frying a bird bigger than your head or an advertisement for wacky party hats.

323

monday
19
32

324

tuesday
20
31

325

wednesday
21
30

326

thursday
22
29

Thanksgiving
Memo: Be thankful you won't have to see this bunch again next year.

327

friday
23
28

328

saturday
24
27

329

sunday
25
26

NOVEMBER

S	M	T	W	T	F	S
				1	2	3
4	5	6	7	8	9	10
11	12	13	14	15	16	17
18	19	20	21	22	23	24
25	26	27	28	29	30	

Notes

THE FORTNIGHTLY GLYPH

STRZ N' B'RZ

Insignia of rebel Southern slavers who traded the demigod **M'Aaz** for **G'Rtz**.

330

monday
26
25

331

tuesday
27
24

332

wednesday
28
23

333

thursday
29
22

334

friday
30
21

335

saturday
1
20

336

sunday
2
19

Advent
Memo: This could be the start of something big.

OH MAYA GOD

A favorite Mayan phrase was *tak samal*, literally "until tomorrow," an early version of the concept of *mañana,* and the response they'd usually get after asking the contractor how soon their sacrificial ziggurat might be finished.

Mayan elders provided a steady diet of feast days, religious observances and three-day holidays honoring every god, demi-god, totemic beast, and magic mushroom distributor they could fit onto the schedule.

Most popular of these was the winter festival of **No'l**, a month-long gift-giving holiday dedicated to the jolly-but-judgmental demi-god **X'anta**. Mayan parents gave presents to their offspring designed to prepare them for adulthood; toy bows and arrows or slabs of granite on which to make sacrifices to **X'bx**, god of games (ages 5 and up). For toddlers there were handcarved **Tickle-Me-Inca** dolls and fetishes of **Fr'b**, avatar of adorableness.

Other important seasonal holidays include:
B'arf — the raucous New Year's celebration overseen by **M'zkal**, deity of spirit visions. Chief activity of this all-night bacchanal was to see how many forms of psychotropic jungle fungi could be distilled into an elixir which would help the believer see the snake god Kukulcan and his imaginary friend, Ollie.

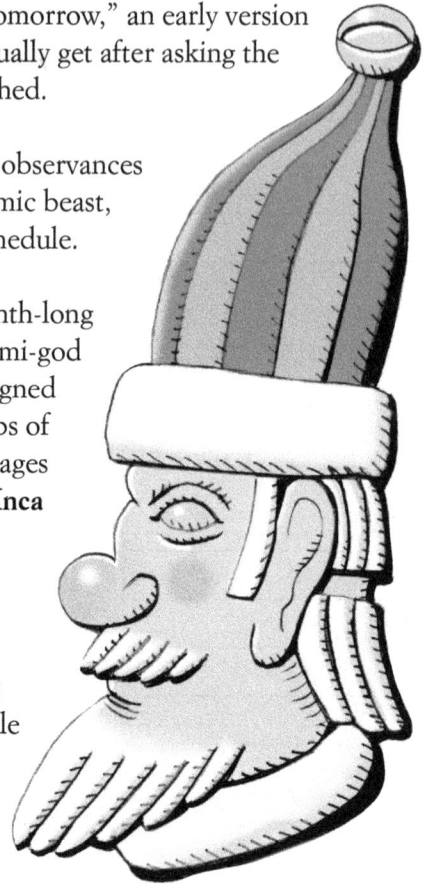

X'ANTA

P'sova — a spring feast day that memorialized the miracle of army ants passing over corn fields without acting meshuga. Celebrants consumed huge meals in honor of **S'dah** and didn't return to work until the feeling of nausea passed over, often after a sacrifice to the spirit **Bz'ml**.

K'rno K'pia — the fall avocado festival honoring the beloved demi-god **G'wok**. The young rode in Toltec slave-drawn carts picking the ripe fruit, while their mothers ground corn meal at home for **ch'ps** to salute the powerful diety **T'ko** — all in anticipation of the first **B'ol*** game of the season.

*See description in March

B'ARF CELEBRANT

December

S	M	T	W	T	F	S
						1
2	3	4	5	6	7	8
9	10	11	12	13	14	15
16	17	18	19	20	21	

No Fly Zone

Flight 19, five Navy torpedo bombers on a training mission — aka *The Lost Squadron* — disappears into the Bermuda Triangle. Spookiest of all, their luggage arrives at the intended destination intact and on time.

THE FORTNIGHTLY GLYPH

E'MOTKON

Only surviving example of its kind, although fragments have been found of **L'OL**, **L'MAO** and **R'OFL**.

337

monday

3

18

338

tuesday

4

17

339

wednesday

5

16

340

thursday

6

15

341

friday

7

14

342

saturday

8

13

Hannukah Begins at Sundown

343

sunday

9

12

December

SEER SUCKERS

Nostradamus is born on this day in 1506. Historians (at least the ones we know) can't say whether Nostradamus was even aware of the Mayans, much less conversant with their calendar, but by an eerie coincidence (or is it?), the word "Nostradamus" in Mayan is slang for, "Mr. Smarty Pants Know It All."

THE FORTNIGHTLY GLYPH

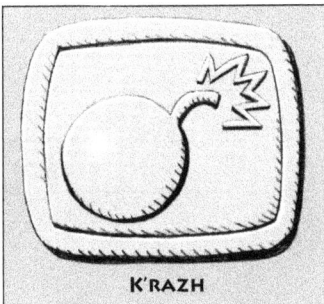

K'RAZH

AKA **K'Boom**; same image also appears on a glyph where it's being held by a wide-eyed coyote.

345

monday
10
11

346

tuesday
11
10

347

wednesday
12
9

348

thursday
13
8

349

friday
14
7

350

saturday
15
6

351

sunday
16
5

Hannukah Ends

December

TO-DO CHECKLIST

√ Replace flashlight batteries.

√ Install extra-thick lead-lined hurricane shutters.

√ Lay in 50-year supply of canned goods.

√ Try to bribe way onto International Space Station.

√ Burn bucket list.

√ Consume case of Cristal.

√ Slash boss's tires.

√ Sleep with spouse's sibling.

√ Max out credit cards.

√ Instruct Post Office to hold mail.

√ Cancel cable.

√ Turn off lights.

352

monday
17
4

353

tuesday
18
3

354

wednesday
19
2

355

thursday
20
1

356

friday
21
0

Winter Solstice
Forecast: Partly cloudy, chance of Doomsday

Final Thoughts

BREAK GLASS
IN CASE OF
DECEMBER 22

December

S	M	T	W	T	F	S
						1
2	3	4	5	6	7	8
9	10	11	12	13	14	15
16	17	18	19	20	21	22
23	24	25	26	27	28	29
30	31					

Undo Checklist

√ List flashlight batteries, extra-thick lead-lined hurricane shutters and 50-year supply of canned goods for sale on eBay.

√ Remove name from International Space Station 'waiting list'.

√ Start new bucket list.

√ Find surefire remedy for Cristal hangover.

√ Create alibi for whereabouts at the time your boss's tires got slashed.

√ Avoid any and all gatherings where sibling and sibling's spouse may be present.

√ Report stolen identity to credit card companies.

√ Think over whether to inform the Post Office that you're still around.

√ Restore cable service; maybe upgrade.

√ Turn lights back on.

OOPS!
SO SORRY
Pardone
Scusi
Gomen nasai
YIKES!
Das tut mir Lied
סליחה

364

saturday
22

365

sunday
23

APOLOGY FORM LETTER FOR BUSINESS

Dear ___1___,

Please regard this as a letter of sincere apology for my recent conduct.

First, let me reiterate that my belief that the world would end on December 21, 2012 was genuine and heartfelt and clearly had a profound effect on my state of mind.

Still, I realize and acknowledge that this does not excuse the incidents regarding my ___2___ behavior or my having ___3___ the ___4___ equipment and my unsavory overtures made towards ___5___ in ___6___.

Obviously, I don't expect to just pick up where I left off ___7___ weeks ago as if nothing had happened, especially after the ___8___, those ___9___ and the unfortunate ___10___ at the ___11___. I am prepared to reimburse the company for the ___12___, ___13___, ___14___, ___15___ (rare, but not, as it turns out, one-of-a-kind), and, of course, you personally for the cost of reconstructing your ___16___. I hope that's coming along nicely and that you'll be able to ___17___ again in the new year.

As a gesture of my sincerity and good faith regarding this matter, I would like to make a generous donation to ___18___.

I hope that we can sit down and discuss all of this as soon as the restraining order is lifted, say, or even sooner if you'd care to rescind it and drop the civil and criminal charges.

Sincerely,

_____
Your Name

December

S	M	T	W	T	F	S
						1
2	3	4	5	6	7	8
9	10	11	12	13	14	15
16	17	18	19	20	21	22
23	24	25	26	27	28	29
30	31					

Suggested Mea Culpas

1: Sir, Madam, World's Greatest Boss

2: inappropriate, sophomoric, sociopathic, (alleged) criminal

3: damaged, burned, soiled, defiled, committed unspeakable acts upon

4: printing, air-conditioning, kitchen, earth-moving, dental

5: that hot babe/hunk [name here], your secretary, your great aunt, your dachshund, Colonel Mustard

6: accounting, the mail room, HR, the ER. the Library

7: [number you'll admit to]

8: fire, oil spill, missing cash, loss of our biggest client, noogie

9: personal insults, charges to the company account, bomb threats, clogged toilets, identity thefts

10: striptease, tantrum, wedgie, feces-flinging, tea-bagging

11: office party, convention, board meeting, company picnic, sink in the executive restroom

12 laptops, missing funds, hookers, candy machine, third floor

13: fax machine, coffee maker, windows, delivery truck, 2013 product line

14: markers, overhead projector, Dom Perignon, strychnine in the water cooler, satellite office

15: office plants, tropical fish, oil painting of Our Founder, Ming vase, secret recipe

16: office wall, lower jaw, collarbone, leg, scrotum

17: walk, breathe normally, eat solid foods, procreate, evacuate your bowels

18: the Red Cross, PETA, your favorite charity, your favorite Swiss bank account, your favorite mistress' plastic surgeon

---

monday
24
Christmas Eve
Memo: Shop like Paris Hilton on meth.

1
tuesday
25
Christmas

2
wednesday
26
Kwanzaa Begins
Boxing Day Canada

3
thursday
27

4
friday
28

5
saturday
29

6
sunday
30

DECEMBER

	S	M	T	W	T	F	S
							1
	2	3	4	5	6	7	8
	9	10	11	12	13	14	15
	16	17	18	19	20	21	22
	23	24	25	26	27	28	29
	30	31					

NEW YEAR'S RESOLUTIONS

1) Lose weight, starting with the 25-ton calendar.

2) Never trust an ancient prophecy unless it mentions you by name (ditto fortune cookies).

3) Drink lots more water and way less mezcal.

4) Read more novels and fewer ancient texts that foretell your extinction.

5) Swear off animal sacrifice.

6) Make looong-term plans.

7) Trade in plumed serpent for Chia Pet.

8) Make 13 your new lucky number, just don't get all weird and mystical about it.

9) Depending on what you did or didn't do in April, find a really good accountant. Maybe a lawyer, too.

10) Recycle, including leftover 2011 resolutions.

366
monday
31

1
tuesday
1
New Year's Day

2
wednesday
2

3
thursday
3

4
friday
4

5
saturday
5

6
sunday
6
Epiphany: Tomorrow is another day.

BUT WAIT! THERE'S MORE!

The end of the Mayan calendar let you down, but just can't shake the doomsday bug? Well, whether you want to put it way off or just get it over with in a hurry, there are plenty more doomsdays to come!

2012

12/23/2012

"Pyramidologist" Graham Hancock laughs at Mayan predictions because he knows that on this date, the Sphinx, UFOs and the pyramids (including the ones on Mars that NASA has been keeping secret from us) will bring about The End.

8/23/2013

According to the Weekly World News, in 1916 Russian "mystic" Rasputin predicted that this date would be the last. Granted, you have to overlook that we've skipped his scheduled preliminaries of Satan's 2002 appearance, deadly plagues in 2003, Jesus' 2005 return and the Loch Ness Monster's coming out party of 2006. Dubious source, you say? Would Bat Boy lie?

12/12/2021

If it turns out that the Mayans were dyslexic, this is the date to watch for.

2025

The Raëlian UFO cult believes its alien pals will arrive this year, after which the rest of us will spend our days polishing our new overlords' tin-foil hats.

2027 – 2039

Jeanne Dixon penciled in this stretch for Armageddon; let's see what movies Jennifer Jason Leigh releases during this time.

3420, 3793, 7000

Dates of doom all attributed to Nostradamus. By whom, you ask? Does it really matter?

1,002,009

Those Chicken Littles at the Jet Propulsion Lab estimate that a hail of comets will make things fairly unpleasant for whatever life form is living in your old house at this point.

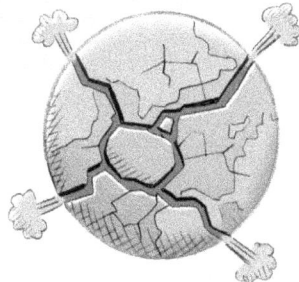

5,000,002,009

The Sun's hydrogen fuses into helium and, despite its voice sounding high-pitched and silly, its core collapses, then, blammo!

THE END

Special Days

January

February

March

April

May

June

Special Days

July

_____
_____
_____
_____
_____
_____
_____
_____
_____
_____

August

_____
_____
_____
_____
_____
_____
_____
_____
_____
_____

September

_____
_____
_____
_____
_____
_____
_____
_____
_____
_____

October

_____
_____
_____
_____
_____
_____
_____
_____
_____
_____

November

_____
_____
_____
_____
_____
_____
_____
_____
_____
_____

December

_____
_____
_____
_____
_____
_____
_____
_____
_____
_____

www.ingramcontent.com/pod-product-compliance
Lightning Source LLC
Chambersburg PA
CBHW081518040426
42447CB00013B/3259